Praise for *The Jo*
and Allison

"Sixteen years of experience improving Massachusetts General Hospital convinced strategic planning and management coach Rimm that achieving personal happiness is not as difficult as it appears. We can give ourselves a kick-start on the path to personal and career satisfaction by designing a business plan for our lives—a process that includes setting core values, identifying goals, and coming up with a strategy for achieving those goals. In her first book, Rimm helps the reader break free from inertia by choosing a mission that encompasses his or her interests and talents, envisioning what success is going to look like, getting past roadblocks, analyzing strengths and weaknesses, and making the most of our most precious commodity: time. Suggestions are supported with accessible and inspiring exercises to help readers figure out what's truly important. While the subject matter is not new, the book makes change seem truly achievable. Readers who feel stuck in their lives will find Rimm's optimism infectious: 'Life is a wild, wondrous adventure and you never know what awaits you around the next bend... Stick to your plans as long as they continue to guide you toward the results you desire.... Have a great trip and keep in touch.'" —*Publishers Weekly*

"This is a fantastic guide to living: well-conceived, beautifully written, filled with wonderful, real-life examples and inspiring messages. Rimm infuses the book with the credo for her own life—to laugh loudly, love deeply, and nourish all with food for thought. *The Joy of Strategy* is truly balm for the soul."

—Suzanne Bates, CEO of Bates Communications, Inc.,
best-selling author of *Speak Like a CEO: Secrets for Commanding Attention and Getting Results*

"One of academia's greatest challenges is mastering the essential art of mentoring. *The Joy of Strategy* not only provides the insight and tools to nurture the extraordinary talents of our young professionals; it demonstrates for mentors how best to mentor. This book should be required reading for organizations that want to reach their full potential."

—Gary Gottlieb, MD, MBA,
president and CEO, Partners HealthCare

"I've had the privilege of seeing Allison Rimm in action. She conveys the *why* for personal strategy development and then the *how* in a very understandable and effective manner. This book is a must-read for anyone who would like to help improve their individual effectiveness in both work and personal aspects of their life."

—James I. Cash, James E. Robison Professor of Business
Administration, Emeritus, Harvard Business School

"This is a wonderful and practical book based on the simple premise that work is only part of our life and that work and life should—make that must—be joyful. You'll find the book loaded with strategies on how to achieve this joy."

—Lawrence Fish, chairman of
Houghton Mifflin Harcourt Corporation

"Having a background in strategic planning, I approached the book with much skepticism, but I became engaged within the first few pages and ultimately became convinced of the importance of having a personal strategic plan. The author's stories and subtle humor bring to life her approach to strategy and make the book a joy to read. Her ideas are enlightening and well-grounded in practice. Her promise of being able 'to focus on what matters most and to spend your time and talent where it can make a meaningful difference' is a compelling reason to undertake a personal strategy development process. In fact, I began to put into practice some of the ideas as soon as I put the book down."

—Raymond V. Gilmartin, former chairman, president, and CEO
of Merck and adjunct professor at Harvard Business School

"Blending a delicious mixture of classic strategic planning techniques, time management tools, and unique life planning exercises, Allison Rimm's *The Joy of Strategy* offers a fresh and compelling method to help people facing a life transition, looking to achieve an ambitious goal, or just stuck in their careers. The special added ingredient comes from an emphasis on seizing joy and happiness along the way. Allison brings her ideas to life with compelling vignettes from her extensive practice, making *The Joy of Strategy* a very authentic and practical guide for a diverse audience. This book will change people's lives!"

—Celia R. Brown, EVP, group human resources director, Willis Group, LTD

"Inspirational leaders know that their primary role is to create and sustain a healthy work environment. This timely book shows readers how to employ the business tools and life lessons Rimm provides to be the leaders of their own balanced and fulfilling lives. She has generously shared her experience, knowledge, and skill, including rich examples of the results people have achieved by putting her techniques into practice. Her work exemplifies leadership at its best. This helpful book provides a wealth of strategies that will help everyone from emerging leaders to seasoned veterans be more effective managing themselves and others."

—Jeanette Ives Erickson, DNP, RN, FAAN, SVP for Patient Care and Chief Nurse at Massachusetts General Hospital and co-author of *Fostering Nurse-Led Care: Professional Practice for the Bedside Leader*

The Joy of Strategy

The Joy of Strategy

of

A Business Plan for Life

Allison Rimm

bibliomotion
books + media

First published by Bibliomotion, Inc.

711 Third Avenue, New York, NY 10017, USA

2 Park Square, Milton Park, Abingdon, Oxon OX14 4RN, UK

Bibliomotion is an imprint of the Taylor & Francis Group, an informa business

Library of Congress Cataloging-in-Publication Data

Rimm, Allison.
   The joy of strategy : a business plan for life / Allison Rimm. — First Edition.
      pages cm
   Includes index.
   ISBN 978-1-937134-55-6 (hardcover : alk. paper) —
ISBN 978-1-937134-56-3 (ebook) — ISBN 978-1-937134-57-0 (enhanced ebook)
   1. Strategic planning.   2. Goal setting in personnel management.   3. Job
satisfaction.   I. Title.
   HD30.28.R556 2013
   650.1—dc23
   2013016000

ISBN-13: 978-1-937-13455-6 (hbk)
ISBN-13: 978-1-629-56142-4 (pbk)

To my grandmother, Frances Hirshon, who taught me what unconditional love really means. And to my mother, Jocelyn Caplan, who personifies grace in adversity and proves that true wisdom doesn't come from a textbook, but from knowing what truly matters and giving it your all.

Contents

Foreword

By Nancy J. Tarbell, M.D.

I first met Allison Rimm when I arrived at Massachusetts General Hospital in 1997 as the new division chief of Pediatric Radiation Oncology and the founding director of the Office for Women's Careers. For many years, she had led hospital-wide strategic planning efforts, rallying hundreds of professionals in the bargain. Allison was also in charge of the Office of the President and served on the committee that created the new department I was hired to lead with the goal of promoting the careers of female faculty at the MGH. From the start, I relied on her expert advice, steadfast advocacy, and ability to get things done in that highly complex organization.

By the time I participated in Allison's groundbreaking course, *The Business of Life: Bringing Organization to Souls* in 2008, I was already a full professor at Harvard Medical School and the founding director of the newly created Office for Faculty Development. I had found my calling and was enjoying a hugely satisfying career treating kids with cancer, leading my division, and helping to develop the careers of the next generation of doctors and scientists.

But I was lucky. I'd never thought of being a doctor until my college friend saw something in me and encouraged me to pursue a career in medicine. It was a moment in a friendship that led me to join the long and hopeful battle to cure children with cancer.

Not everyone is so fortunate to have such an insightful—and forceful—friend. All around me, family, friends, and acquaintances, seemed to be juggling so many commitments that they were utterly exhausted, yet many of them expressed that they didn't feel like much of that activity really mattered much in the long run.

At work, several of my peers and much of the junior faculty were struggling with all manner of professional challenges while also trying to have a family and maintain some sense of sanity in the process. This was especially true for the women faculty who, despite the tentative progress we'd made in gender equality, were still primarily responsible for childcare and household administration in addition to their responsibilities at work. It was in my heart, and my job description, to help them reach their professional goals and find some semblance of work/life balance.

Allison's course not only offered us all a strategic framework to approach managing our careers and our lives, it gave us the time, space, and guidance to consider what was truly important to us and the tips, tools, and techniques necessary to make progress on the most essential initiatives. But she didn't stop there. She blended her skills as a strategist with soulful wisdom and gave us permission to think about what made us joyful at work and at home. Now, that was a first in the highly traditional world of academic medicine! But if you stop to really think about it, doctors—or anyone for that matter—who are happy at work and thriving in their careers will bring that sense of joy into the examining room when they see patients. They will bring it to their laboratories, administrative roles, and any other endeavors they pursue. And that positive attitude fuels their ability to be effective in their many roles.

But that doesn't just happen. Finding fulfillment and satisfaction requires that we have the tools and know-how needed to set priorities, manage our time, and cope with our own habits that stand in the way of us achieving our goals and enjoying the process. Over the years, Allison has shared the tricks of the trade that helped her rise to her senior leadership position in one of the world's most highly esteemed institutions with hundreds of faculty and staff at the MGH through her Business of Life courses. With her warm, candid, and compassionate approach to teaching solid self-management and project management skills, Allison created an environment where the people felt safe to express their deepest professional concerns and their career ambitions. And then they helped each other address their challenges by sharing their own stories with one another.

Perhaps the most profound shift in the classroom took place when these faculty-turned-students gave themselves the credit they deserved for achieving what they had accomplished already and cultivated some patience with themselves as they faced their next challenge. It was wonderful to witness the optimism—and relief—they experienced when they learned about the concrete steps they could take to achieve the results they desired. While I wish I had thought about some of these things earlier in my own career, I was glad to have had the opportunity to offer this experience to our faculty *and* be a participant.

In the *The Joy of Strategy*, Allison has recreated that space where her readers can learn her novel approach to thinking about their lives and careers strategically. This book is readable, entertaining, and provides practical, doable step-by-step guidance to make a business plan for your life. These principles come alive with the stories of people who have used these techniques to solve problems and make their dreams come true. All the while, Allison maintains a focus on finding some daily pleasures while working toward longer-term goals.

Anyone who cares about using their talents to do something meaningful with their lives should grab a notebook, read this book, and complete the exercises in it. Then they should create a plan and make it happen. Reading the *The Joy of Strategy* is a great first step.

Dr. Nancy J. Tarbell is the Dean for Academic and Clinical Affairs and the C.C. Wang Professor of Radiation Oncology at Harvard Medical School. She is a longstanding advocate for faculty development initiatives including mentoring programs for junior faculty and numerous efforts on behalf of women and minorities.

Acknowledgments

For a pursuit as solitary as writing, it's remarkable how many people have contributed to bringing this work into being. During the writing phase, my thoughts vacillated between moments of panic and "pinch me!" wonder at how lucky I am to have so many people in my corner.

First, my deepest gratitude goes to my all my friends and family for your love, patience, and encouragement. I must mention just a few: Jeri Weiss is my amazing alter ego and Matt Goldman our treasured co-conspirator. Alma Berson offered endless shots of courage. Meir and Claire Stampfer hosted countless dinners and made sure my family never starved for company or sustenance.

I am thankful to my coaching and consulting clients and the thousands of people who have attended my lectures and participated in my workshops, seminars, and courses. You have taught me so much and your accomplishments motivated me to write this book. I'm honored to have played a small part in your journey. I am particularly grateful to those of you whose stories appear on these pages. Thank you for serving as role models and inspiring others.

Finding my voice as a writer was a high hurdle and I couldn't have cleared it without Louisa Kasden and Donna Frazier Glynn. Jennifer Caplan and Willow Clark were among the first to read early chapters and gave me the courage to show them to others and Ellen Alfaro gave me the gift of her company on a writing retreat.

Andy O'Connell, my friend, and Harvard Business Review editor patiently challenged me to refine my message, always keeping the readers' needs in mind. His insights have been invaluable.

A gigantic thank you to everyone who read each chapter and provided priceless comments: Jennifer Caplan, Ellen Alfaro, Eric Rimm, Hannah Rimm, Sara Rimm-Kaufman, Trudy Craig, Alma Berson, and Bob Malster. Carey Goldberg must be singled out here for providing the most expert, insightful, and compassionate editorial advice anyone could hope for. I'd be more emphatic about her contributions, but she allows no exclamation points.

Of course, writing the book wasn't enough. Finding the right publisher was essential and it took a village. Thanks to Karla Todd who introduced me to Stacy DeBroff who introduced me to Lisa Butler who introduced me to Kate Sweetman who led me to Madelyn Sierra who introduced me to Carolyn Monaco who persistently pushed me to contact the extraordinary Erika Heilman. I can't imagine a better group than the gang at Bibliomotion: Erika, her co-founder and president, Jill Friedlander, Jill Schoenhaut, Susan Lauzau, Susanna Kellogg, Emily Hanson, and Shevaun Betzler. It's a joy to be a part of your spectacular community.

Dr. Jim Cash has been an important, generous mentor. Countless others have kindly shared their experiences and expertise. I could never list them all, but trust they know how much they mean to me. Thanks to my associates past and present, especially Peggy Meehan, Manny Correia, Lee Ann Ross, Bonnie Michelman, and Mary Finlay.

Finally, no one endured more "stuff" than those who lived with me while I wrote (and wrote and wrote). Hannah and Isaac's notes of encouragement grace the walls of my tiny office. Their many "mini-visits" just to say hi or plant a kiss were precious. Eric Rimm, my cherished husband and partner in life, patiently reassured me over and over, and was constantly available to serve as a sounding board. If that isn't enough, he makes me laugh every day. His support and friendship blow me away. I can't imagine traveling this road without him.

Introduction

What Is a Strategic Plan and Why Do You Need One?

The joy of a life well lived—our work well done, our cherished ones well loved, our potential realized. Isn't that what we're all after? You don't need to leave your dreams to chance. However, achieving this most fundamental and often elusive goal doesn't just happen. It requires a strategy. To create a meaningful plan, you need a structured approach that guides you, step by step, through the process of defining what is most important to you and what you must do to get it. The world's most successful businesses do this as a matter of course, and there is no more essential business than the business of your life.

Here's my story. In 1995, I was recruited to lead Massachusetts General Hospital, the nation's top-ranked hospital,[1] through a strategic planning process and bring order to the chaos that was the chief executive's office. Chaos at MGH? Doesn't everyone know that stands for Man's Greatest Hospital? From the outside, everything looked great for this world-renowned institution and, for the most part, it was. But as the health care industry rapidly changed around it, the formula that brought this prestigious medical center legendary success for nearly two centuries would send them into a slow death spiral if they didn't develop a strategy to thrive in the evolving landscape.

While the hospital worked to position itself for continued success in the new millennium, the CEO was seriously overcommitted. His calendar was consistently over-booked and he needed a system to ensure he spent his time on matters that required his personal attention.

More than that, in this time of unprecedented change, he needed to improve communications with the hundreds of clinical and administrative leaders who had to carry out this new agenda *and* reduce the time they spent in meetings so they could get this extra work done while providing the exceptional patient care for which they were so well known. Like the hospital he was tasked to run, he needed a strategic plan of his own.

While we didn't call it that at the time, that CEO was my first coaching client. He urgently needed to set priorities and make his actions reflect them. He had to stop allowing his assistant to overbook his calendar and I told him so during my job interview. So when the request came in for him to attend a vendor selection meeting for their computer system during our interview, he turned to me and asked if he should accept. I told him if he didn't have people he could count on to attend that meeting and give him a recommendation he could trust, he was in bigger trouble than he thought. He offered me the job that very day. Thus began my sixteen-year stint running the executive office for him and the two presidents who followed.

Your Joy in Jeopardy

Chances are you are a lot like this CEO, highly accomplished in your own way and with so many demands coming at you that it's hard to get through the day in one piece, let alone feeling fulfilled and joyful. As a person with your own unique gifts to offer, it is your responsibility to use your talents wisely and it is your right to enjoy yourself while doing so. Happiness is so fundamental, in fact, that its pursuit is even stated as a right in the United States' Declaration of Independence. Yet despite achieving phenomenal career successes, countless professionals are experiencing feelings ranging from vague dissatisfaction to utter misery.

As a senior executive and management consultant, I'm astonished that more leaders don't pay close attention to how their employees *feel* about their work, or at least they don't do this formally. To put it in economic terms, I've come to appreciate over the years that happiness on the job is a leading indicator of an individual's ability to sustain high levels of passion, performance, and productivity over the long run. Because any organization's greatest asset is the people who work there, supporting joy on the job seems an obvious way to protect that investment.

This just makes intuitive sense to me—so much so that I even invented a metric and an instrument to measure it. Productivity indicators for individual performance are common, as are profitability measures for organizations. I also track people's joy quotient, which is simply a measure of the joy-to-hassle ratio of a given situation. And I measure it on my joy meter, which I keep in my office. When I worked in the executive suite of Mass General Hospital, countless people would come into my office, close the door, and point the dial on my meter toward hassle or joy, depending on what had happened recently. You'd be surprised by the number of very senior, world-famous physicians who have had a go at it.

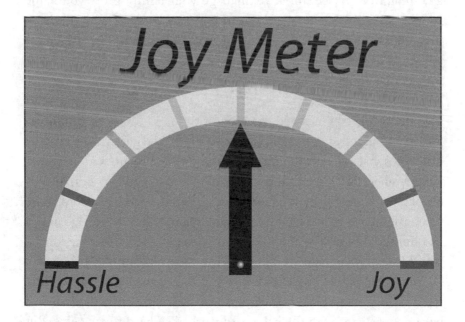

With so many experts exhorting us to work smarter, not harder, why are so many smart people working so hard? Even smart people need help. Like the overcommitted CEO, they need a solid framework to guide decisions large and small. In this book, I will be your coach as you create a business plan for your life so you can enjoy success on your own terms. This eight-step process mirrors the strategic planning steps that may be quite familiar to you, but here we will mix in some tools that may surprise you to bring you joy *and* success. I will teach you some hard skills to accomplish this and will offer firm but gentle guidance to support you when the work itself is tough.

Self-Management and More

The great news about learning how to create a business plan for your life is that you can apply this newfound knowledge so you can be more effective in everything you do. Beyond managing yourself, you will be better equipped to lead teams and projects at work, rally the troops for a community service initiative, manage your family life—you name it. The investment you are about to make in yourself will pay huge dividends for the rest of your life and in ways that may surprise you.

The Time for Your Passions Is Now

Helping such a complex and historic institution as MGH determine its future was an intriguing intellectual challenge. And gaining the support of the hospital's leaders to implement the resulting plan, with its inevitable winners and losers, called on all of my diplomatic skills and powers of persuasion. My accomplishments were rewarded with more: more responsibility, more people to lead, and larger budgets to manage until I had hundreds of people and tens of millions of dollars under my direction. More of what many professionals regard as indicators of success.

And then came the year that changed everything. After enduring a string of heart-wrenching personal losses, I was thrilled when I became pregnant with the baby we'd worked so hard to conceive. But elation turned quickly to fear when we learned his heart didn't appear to be developing properly and it was not clear if he would survive. We had to make some impossibly difficult decisions. If that wasn't enough, in the midst of that pregnancy, my husband was diagnosed with a potentially life-threatening condition that required a risky surgery to repair. Facing the very real possibility that I could lose the husband and child I cherished so deeply, I realized our time was short and I needed to make the most of it—*now*.

That meant leading with my heart and emotional intelligence after years of putting my intellectual gifts first. I'd spent my life thinking that if I worked hard enough I could fulfill my potential: put myself through college; earn a graduate degree from Harvard; effectively manage huge projects and successful teams; and win big contracts, awards, and promotions; and I did all that. Yet, at the pinnacle of my career, I knew that snuggling up with big budgets wasn't enough and that my real satisfaction came from connecting deeply with other people and making a positive difference. After a great deal of introspection, I realized that my unique ability to combine the techniques I'd employed so effectively in business with some hard-won life lessons to help others to find soul-satisfying success was a great way to do that. So while mixing soul with strategy isn't exactly the most intuitive combination, it is a lot more spiritual than leaving your dreams to chance or, worse, letting them go because you don't know how to pursue them. I've met a lot of souls that need organizing. More than that, many organizations need soul. After conducting dozens of workshops for people ranging from physicians to firefighters, I could see that using my strategic planning and executive skills was the perfect way to put my passion into practice.

What Is a Strategic Plan and Why Do You Need One?

"Good plans shape good decisions. That's why good planning helps make elusive business dreams come true."[2]

—Lester Robert Bittel, industrial engineer
and management guru

In its simplest form, strategic planning is the process of identifying your purpose and core values, setting goals, and developing the approach that is most likely to achieve them. A strategic plan serves as a road map that defines your destination and shows how you can use your talents to take you there. Several routes are possible, and this map lays out which way is most likely to get you there quickly and reliably.

Are you thinking this just isn't for you and that you might put down this book? Not so fast! I've seen time and again that the people who resist this process are the very people who need it most. If the term strategic planning makes you think "I'd rather have a colonoscopy," rest assured I will walk you through a focused, streamlined process aimed at giving you practical news you can use and not a bunch of jargon-filled fluff. Drawing a map that takes you someplace you actually want to go requires some careful thought and quiet reflection. Working with this book, you will create the space that makes that possible.

> *"I went to the woods because I wished to live deliberately, to front only the essential facts of life, and to see if I could not learn what it had to teach, and not, when I came to die, discover that I had not lived."*[3]
> —Henry David Thoreau, *Walden*, 1854

No business could attract investors without clearly stating what its purpose is and what it hopes to achieve. Further, backers would not be satisfied by a fledgling business "hoping" to fulfill its mission: they require a detailed business plan showing the specific actions the business will take to accomplish what it sets out to do. In the business world, no one is going to take an uncalculated risk. Savvy investors know how to pick a winner, and winners have a clear sense of where they are going and how they are going to get there. Furthermore, their plans are doable and have a high degree of probability that they will yield the results needed for a successful return on investment.

Asset Management

Once you have gotten clear about what you want to achieve, you can be a responsible steward of your limited resources—time, money, talents—and utilize your assets in ways that are most likely to get you the results you desire.

Your Life Is Serious Business…

Just like that business, *you* need a clear picture of what you want to accomplish and what success means for you in order to focus your efforts and achieve your goals. Don't leave fulfilling your dreams to chance. If you don't take the time to decide where you want to go, it is impossible to draw a map that will help you reach your destination. Lacking direction, you could spend endless days simply responding to what others want from you. Years of this condition can leave you feeling unfulfilled and asking "Is this all there is?"

So You Need a Business Plan for Life

Most people don't live deliberately and they skip the critical step of deciding what is most important before they act, a state Thoreau sought to avoid for himself with his reflective sojourn in Walden Woods. Without a clearly defined purpose, many people find they are not living their lives. Their lives are living *them*. Your own strategic plan is the result of a structured, systematic process and provides you with the basis from which you can make good decisions, both personal and professional.

Step off the Treadmill and Break Free from Inertia

Let me tell you about Danielle. In the first several years we knew each other, I rarely saw her fully dressed and never saw her completely happy. Our lockers were located close together at our health club and we chatted every morning as we dressed to go off to work. We would discuss what was ahead of us that day and quip about funny things that we'd seen at the gym.

While I'd usually be excited about a talk I was giving or an interesting client I'd be meeting, Danielle was not so enthusiastic. She worked in the fashion industry and would often regale me with outrageous tales of her company's dysfunction. While her stories were devilishly funny, they revealed how truly miserable she was. Her job was eating away at her spirit and each day she dreaded going to work. The problems only compounded when her company was bought out and a new management team took over.

One morning, Danielle came into the gym more excited than I'd seen her in months. She and her colleagues were going to be laid off at the end of the summer and if she stayed with the company until the agreed-upon date, she would get a sizable bonus. The end was in sight.

She was counting the days until she could leave when she showed up at the gym one day deflated. Her new manager told her she was needed to help with the transition. While she was desperate to leave the company, she needed the bonus to give her time to pursue new career options. Over the ensuing months, as this demand was repeated and she was promised ever-growing bonuses, she stayed even longer. During this period, she was contacted about a senior position in a competing company and was actually considering pursuing another job in the industry she couldn't wait to leave.

It was clear to me that Danielle was allowing herself to be swept away by the inertia brought about by circumstances rather than taking the lead role in her life and writing her own script. I suggested she participate in the Business of Life workshop I was giving later that month and she gratefully accepted. This day would allow her to sit back and think about what was really important to her. With that in mind, she could consider how this decision would impact her life and whether it was a wise move. She had never stepped off the treadmill long enough to see how the decisions she was making impacted her health, relationships, and general sense of joy and purpose. In order to do that she needed a plan, and this workshop was just the opportunity she needed to take charge of her own well-being. We will meet up with Danielle later in this book to see the changes she made.

Get Clarity and Get Going

There's nothing mysterious or overly complicated about this kind of planning and strategizing. But for many people, it's the missing piece, the step-by-step breakdown that shows them very concretely what they need to do to put their own dreams first every day and how to find effective strategies to deal with what's derailed them in the past.

Those who achieve *soul-satisfying* success don't rely on intellect alone. These people know that to be truly happy, they need to focus on what's most important. They have more than a high IQ. They have a plan. A strategic plan. I know because I've taught them how to create one. They are smart enough to know what they don't know and they're not afraid to ask directions. They have attended my workshops and courses or have hired me as their coach. And you are about to learn what they have discovered.

This book guides you through that process, which begins by connecting you with your deepest life purpose and then walks you through bringing that ideal into reality. It's not just about visualizing. It's also about looking carefully at what you have, what you need, and how to get it. A strategic plan, unlike other things you may have tried (vision boards, simple lists, resolutions), helps you create strategies for moving steadily toward your target—based on who you really are, strengths, weaknesses, and all.

If you're worried that this work will take some of that precious time you just don't have, rest assured that once you sharpen your tools, your future efforts will be far more precise and efficient. As Melissa, an operations manager and early graduate of this program, said, "The best thing about your class is how timeless everything was. It was such a great investment of time because I still use your techniques [five years later] for goal setting all the time and I know I always will. It's just the way I think now." You will see how Melissa employed these techniques at work and at home with relative ease and achieved her two most important goals—getting promoted and finding a husband—in short order.

Zen Garden in the Shark Tank

Predictably, as I rose through the ranks at MGH, ultimately becoming a senior vice president, more and more people sought me out for coaching and mentoring. It's very satisfying to help earnest, able professionals advance their careers and enjoy life outside of work and I was glad to do it. MGH is blessed with countless bright and dedicated professionals contributing to its worthy mission. Yet even in such a rich environment, the uncompromising drive for excellence can be daunting and stressful, taking its toll over time. My office became known as an oasis of serenity in the hospital's relentlessly fast-paced environment as I guided people to make choices that brought them professional *and* personal satisfaction.

If the notion of monitoring people's joy on the job sounds frivolous to you, I have some outcomes of my own that validate the utility of paying close attention to your employees' happiness and engagement in their work. In my sixteen years at MGH, not a single one of my department heads left the institution. In fact, up until a few months before I left, there was zero turnover among my direct reports. That one change occurred when the hospital CIO was promoted to lead the IT enterprise for our entire system, a move I heartily endorsed. That loyalty and longevity doesn't just happen.

If these empirical data aren't enough to convince you, a recent study by Dr. Michal Biron of the University of Haifa's Graduate School of Management showed that employees are less likely to take time off for stress-related illnesses when they receive "emotional and instrumental support" from their supervisors. Absenteeism due to stress-related illnesses cost U.S. businesses an estimated $225.8 billion annually.[4] If you need a reason to support your workers, there are a quarter trillion good ones right there.

When the demand for individual mentoring sessions rose beyond what my calendar allowed, I created a course to teach groups of leaders the skills they needed to manage their careers and their lives. The course, called The Business of Life, was instantly oversubscribed and the classes have been full ever since. As word spread, I developed courses for the doctors and research faculty at the hospital and created programs for my coaching and consulting clients in financial services, broadcasting, marketing, higher education, government, and a wide variety of other industries.

Recently, I met with a group of physicians and surgeons who had taken my course six weeks earlier to check in on how they were putting their new knowledge into action. In spite of being brilliant and virtuous doctors, or maybe because of that, they had been feeling pretty dissatisfied. After just one day of learning about the Business of Life, they were able to make small changes in their habits that made a huge impact on their outlook and experience. They felt more in control. More like they were running the show rather than the show running them. Here are just a few examples of what they had to say about their experience:

- "It was life changing."
- "I let go of trying to do everything. Your challenging me to ask myself, 'what would happen if this doesn't get done' was so eye opening. Often, the answer was 'not much,' and sometimes even 'I can do something that is much more important.' So basic. Why hadn't I figured that out long ago?"
- "This experience completely changed the lens I look through when evaluating work requests. I allowed myself to feel anger for the first time when a colleague tried to dump his work on me instead of worrying about how I was going to please him. And for the first time, I simply said no. I was shocked when all he said was 'OK, I'll try someone else.' Sh*t, that's liberation!"

It is so fulfilling to hear how people have used what they've learned in my classes over the years not only to transform their own lives, but also to do amazing things that help countless others in myriad ways. I knew I needed to broaden my reach so even more people can do the same. That defines my mission. I've written this book to coach you through the process of creating a business plan for your life so you can fulfill your potential and make your own special contribution.

Who Will Benefit from This Book?

The beauty of this process is that it meets you where you are and takes you where you want to go. Whether you are looking to find direction and transform your life, fine-tune an otherwise pretty good life, or just figure out how to manage your time so you can get home for dinner by six every night, you will find help reaching your goal. If you are looking for a new job or more satisfaction from the one you already have, you will find tools and suggestions on these pages.

You will take from this process what you need. That was made very clear to me the first time I taught the Business of Life workshop in a large company. At the end of the course, several people came up to the podium to thank me for such an enriching experience. First in line was the manager of the company's parking garage. He said, "That was the best time management class I've ever had." The very next person in line declared that "this was a life-altering experience," and the tools he'd learned helped him and his wife make some major life decisions after they had already achieved their career goals. You will see the results Bruce accomplished later in this book.

As a strategic planner, of course I believe everyone should have a life plan, one that balances career, relationships, mind/body/spirit, and community service priorities. My programs have been enormously popular with professionals across a wide range of disciplines and industries. Business leaders often find that sharing my methods with their staff helps with team bonding and makes them more effective at assigning people to the roles that play to their strengths and ignite their passion at work. People from all walks of life have benefitted from my workshops, often at times of transition such as career shifts, nests emptying, and retirement, to name a few. I frequently hear from course participants that they've shared their materials with a spouse or a friend. Who wouldn't benefit from taking a careful look at her life so she can make conscious, well-considered choices?

Left and Right Brains Unite

One thing that is so appealing about the strategic planning process is that it works for just about everyone. Some people love the conceptual work and find that creating a vision comes naturally, but the practical steps to bring it to life often elude them. Others, who are more left-brain and analytically oriented, are quite comfortable making lists and getting things done. For them, the challenge is focusing on the big questions like their life's purpose so they can be sure all those completed tasks contribute to their most meaningful goals. If life planning has fallen short for you in the past, it is probably because you neglected half the story.

After decades of working with people all along that spectrum, I can warn you right now, parts of this process may well put you a bit outside of your comfort zone and you may find yourself resisting certain activities. Do them anyway. The parts that are hardest for you are likely the ones that will have the biggest payoff—much like exercising when you're out of shape. It's not easy, but you know this investment will make you stronger. And after some practice, it becomes much more natural.

Some Artists Take the First Step

Peggy and Gail are artists with a burning desire to inspire "peace, spirit, and healing" in a supportive environment for children and teens touched by cancer. As breast cancer survivors, they were struck by how isolating it is to be so sick and also by the way the medical system cured their disease but left them on their own to heal their souls.

As artists, they had no trouble visualizing how they could help these kids, but they had no idea how to start the practical tasks of making it come about. I taught them the fundamentals of developing a strategic plan and coached them to start with one small action that very first day. I sent them off with the simple assignment of buying some beautiful folders and a colorful rack that appealed to their aesthetic so they could file away all their papers. Now they had an office set up. It was starting to look real. They were surprised by how quickly small, concrete actions added up to tangible results. You will watch their Our Space, Inc. story unfold throughout this book.

Ticked off Tasks Don't Add Up

Stan is a coaching client whose work life defined the term "rat race." He started working right out of business school, where he'd gone for that most practical reason: he wanted to make money. That he has done. And like a lot of people, once he set out on his path, way back in his early twenties, he never changed course or even gave much thought to what he really wanted to do with his life. There was no time for that. He spent nonstop days reacting to the fast-paced drama of the stock-trading floor. The problem was, after the first few years, none of that activity ever added up to anything he cared about.

Like Danielle, Stan got the shock and opportunity of a lifetime when he was downsized right out of his rut. At first, losing his job seemed like a crisis. But then, he used that "crisatunity" to refocus— or maybe to focus on the big questions for the first time.

How This Book Is Organized

Over the years, I have streamlined the strategic planning process to address the most essential elements you need to consider to achieve your goals efficiently. I keep it simple because the work it guides is not easy. We start with simple exercises so you can ease in and gain confidence as the complexity of the tasks grows. You will see stories every step of the way that illustrate how real people have used this program to address all kinds of goals and challenges. The names and/or details in some of these examples have been altered to maintain anonymity or to illustrate a specific point. In a few cases, the characters presented are composites of more than one individual.

I will be your guide as you work through my 8-Step Strategic Planning Program. In each section, you will complete exercises to accomplish all the necessary steps. You will find tools you can gather to address your particular needs and assemble your own custom toolbox. We start with an assessment of who you are, what you care about, where you want to go, and how well you're positioned to get there. You will do some organized, strategic soul-searching.

Step 1—Mission: Find Your Purpose
Step 2—Vision: Imagine the Sweet Smell (Sound, Look, and Feel) of Success
Step 3—Name Your Critical Success Factors: What You Need to Succeed
Step 4—Find Your Sweet SWOT

From here, we move from who you *are* to what you're going to *do* to express your essential self, employing your talents and putting your passions into play.

Step 5—Set Goals: What You Need to Do to Get the Results You Desire

Next, we do some diagnosis: how well are your activities aligned with your goals? Where are you off track and why?

Step 6—Perform a Time and Emotion Study

Finally, you will find treatments for whatever is standing between you and your goals—practical advice and tools to help you choose the strategies that are most likely to get you the results you want. You will learn new ways to excavate time from your calendar to invest in your most worthy pursuits. You will find tips and tools to help you get back on track if you find you've strayed off the path. The process ends with you devising an action plan that will break down your next steps into bite-sized, doable pieces that banish procrastination and set you in motion toward your vibrant future. Today.

Step 7—Select Successful Strategies
Step 8—Get Going! Your Simplementation Plan
Step Back—Tips and Tools to Get Back on Track and Stay the Course

How You Will Work with This Book

You are about to get very organized. You will also eliminate the anxiety that comes from trying to keep myriad details in your head by putting everything on paper. For this, you will need a notebook to record your thoughts and complete the exercises. Then, you will organize the most critical pieces into a one-page designer document that will make it easy for you to track your progress regularly and make timely course corrections.

Your Custom Closet

Ask anyone in the know what the greatest pitfall of strategic planning is and she will likely say it's when a company spends tons of time and money creating a huge, impenetrable document that gets put aside and collects dust.

Well, this isn't another plan to put on the shelf—it *is* the shelf.

I will confess to being an organization junkie to the point that cleaning out my closets gives me a sense of order when life feels like it's getting out of control. So it seems an apt metaphor to use a custom closet to organize the essential elements of our life plan. You can use this to clear out the clutter of your life, eliminate anything that no longer fits or that blocks your view of the clothes you'd rather wear each day, and make space for new ideas and priorities. With your essentials

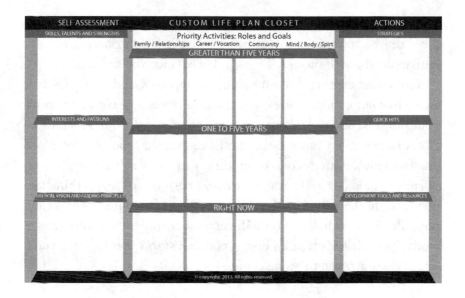

easily visible, you can try mixing and matching them in new, intriguing combinations.

Okay, I can almost hear you snickering at my obsessive devotion to getting organized, but this isn't just about indulging my infatuation with the velvet-lined jewelry drawers you can build into those high-end closets. According to Merriam-Webster's online dictionary,[5] the word *organize* means "to form into a coherent unity or functioning whole." Isn't that what we're after? Aren't we all seeking the integrity that comes when what we do is in harmony with what we believe so that we feel balanced and whole? Organizing ourselves is critical to making that happen.

I just Googled the term "work–life balance" and it returned 208 *million* results. That's a serious problem. I believe the reason that work–life balance is so elusive is that our definition of balance is fundamentally flawed. If you, like so many, are looking to allocate the "right" number of hours to work versus life activities, you've set up a false dichotomy and an equation that can't be solved. My friends, life *is* work. Keeping your house clean, staying fit, and maintaining healthy relations all require work. But work doesn't necessarily suggest drudgery. Your work—at the office or on behalf of your community, health, or home life—can be rewarding, joyful even, when it is contributing to your individual vision of success. That kind of balance you can achieve.

Your closet captures your mission, vision, goals, and strategies, balanced by your own priorities, and it will serve as an easy way to track your progress and course correct for years to come. And it's a custom closet because you can use the shell I've created (you can download one from joyofstrategy.com) or modify it in any way that serves your purposes. Laid out in the way that works best for you, everything you need is right there in one place. Can't get to one of your priorities right now? Put it on a shelf so you will remember to get to it when you're ready. Now that it's written down, you can stop worrying that you'll forget about it when the time comes.

Your Toolbox

This book is full of news you can use. Sprinkled throughout are Toolboxes that you can use to address challenges you may be facing at any point throughout the process. You will also find many tips and techniques to help you get and stay on a fruitful path toward achieving your goals. Whenever any of these speaks to you, you can record them in your notebook or put them on a shelf in your closet so they are available for ready access whenever you need them.

Reservoirs of Joy Create Resilience

I thought I was organized until Lauren, a Wall Street analyst and consulting client, showed up to our first meeting with a file full of color-coded folders, one for each topic we were to cover and another summarizing all of the research she'd conducted to back up every point we'd address in her organization's strategic plan. You can imagine that two methodical planners hit it off and we became great friends once she'd launched her successful strategy.

Over lunch about a year later, she confessed that she had been skeptical about "the joy thing." While she had nodded politely when I described that part of my approach, she was secretly thinking, "*I* don't need that," and dug into the project in earnest when we got to the "real" work. So it was a true gift when she told me that some part of her had absorbed the message. She was concerned that her tween-aged son was too serious and worked too hard. As they planned his summer activities, she remembered about those reservoirs of joy I'd mentioned and she shipped him off to spend the summer with relatives in Europe with nothing but good times with good people on the agenda. She was thrilled when he returned from his visit with his crazy cousins with an easy laugh and quick wit he'd rarely demonstrated before his trip. These qualities eased his transition to high school, where he easily made new friends. And he was a lot more fun at the dinner table, a bonus Lauren truly treasured.

Lauren realized that her son's time in Europe had created joyful memories that he could draw on when he returned to the pressure of his schoolwork. And when he needed a break, he could relieve some stress with a good chortle. She was sold.

These reservoirs of joy make us more resilient dealing with the daily stresses we all face. Have you ever noticed that you can put up with tedious tasks when you are surrounded by colleagues you respect and enjoy? Or that your annoying coworkers don't bother you so much when your work is enormously fulfilling? That's your joy quotient in action: the joy you feel offsets the inevitable hassles you have to face. And having a deep reservoir to call on will help take you through the joy drought brought about by a particularly difficult situation. That's another way you can capture that sense of balance that eludes so many.

Don't Die with Your Song Still Inside You

When I was in the third grade, my music teacher, Mr. Series, directed me to stand in the back row of the chorus and silently mouth the words to the song we were rehearsing for the winter concert. With that one dismissive act, he extinguished the enthusiasm of an exuberant (if not tonally superior) student who had, moments before, been singing with gusto and glee.

Decades later, just after my fortieth birthday, I was sitting in the audience of a concert at a national convention where my daughter's musical ensemble had been invited to sing with the choir. As several musical luminaries joined one another to jam onstage and make beautiful music, I thought wistfully how tragic it was that I loved to sing so much and couldn't carry a tune. Then a lightbulb went on over my forty-year-old head as I realized that I hadn't yet done everything possible to develop my singing ability and that the real tragedy would be to have had the raw talent all along without ever knowing it or developing it. So, I resolved that day to give it my best shot before giving up on something that would bring me so much joy.

That week, I registered for a weekend-long workshop that promised to "have you singing the way you've always wanted to" and that "not an ounce of talent" was required. It took every bit of courage I could summon to mount the stage and sing in front of a group of strangers, but I was determined not to die with my song still inside me, quite literally.

The leader of my singing workshop saw the reticent little third grade girl Mr. Series had silenced so many years ago now standing onstage, choking on my fears and croaking out a feeble tune. He saw that I had to get out of my own way and told me to try again, this time pretending to be a New York City truck driver. I dropped my register and belted out like a tough guy used to shouting at other drivers at the top of his lungs. The crowd laughed and sang along and then jumped to their feet cheering when I triumphantly finished my song.

Shame on Mr. Series for not doing his job: teaching that eager third grader how to sing on key. But as an adult, I am responsible for my own experience. What's holding you back from pursuing your dreams? If it's that you don't know how to start, or are stuck, your excuses are gone. I challenge you to defy any limiting beliefs and to take decisive action toward making those dreams come true. Don't die with your song still inside you.

Step ❶

Mission: Find Your Purpose

"Hide not your talents, they for use were made: What's a sun-dial in the shade?"[1]

—Benjamin Franklin

Every great strategic plan starts with a declaration of an entity's purpose that expresses why it exists, what its members value, and what these people intend to accomplish. Your mission is nothing short of your purpose here on earth, and you'll start your personal plan by spelling it out. I know that sounds lofty, as though we're trying to find the meaning of life. But the answer to the question "What am I here to do?" isn't as remote as you might think. What do you love to do? What are you good at? You'll find your mission right there—it's as accessible and profound as that. I love author Matthew Kelly's definition of what we're after: "Mission is where our talents and passions collide with the needs of others and the world."[2]

Wouldn't it be reassuring, when you are making decisions, to have a filter that separates what is important from what is not? That's what a good mission statement can do for you, and creating one is the first step in engaging your heart and mind in making a plan to fulfill your most deeply held desires.

As with any organization, if you don't have clear intentions, you will have great difficulty focusing your efforts to achieve a *deliberate* result. Something will happen, all right, but you may not like it. Lack of clear direction is the reason so many of us career from task to task, collapsing in an exhausted heap at the end of the day feeling like we haven't really accomplished anything of value. So how can you get ahead of the daily deluge of incoming demands and opportunities and focus on what's truly important? You need to start with knowing your own purpose, what matters most to you.

Mission Critical

While you may find it tempting to dismiss talking about abstractions such as defining your purpose as, well, abstract, discussing your intentions actually leads to very practical actions. Defining your mission is critical to allocating your resources, time, and abilities wisely.

This was evident when I was assigned the task of solving a problem that had plagued Massachusetts General Hospital's Board of Trustees for years. The trustees wanted to feel more closely connected to this esteemed institution and to make better use of their legendary expertise. The board is a treasure trove of talent that includes captains of industry, bank presidents, a National Football League team owner and a Major League Baseball team owner, leading academics, philanthropists, and community leaders. But when they came together for board meetings, the management team spent so much time presenting vast amounts of information that the trustees reported it was like trying to drink from a fire hose. Furthermore, there was little, if any, time left for discussion, so the trustees didn't feel like they were making much of a contribution. And they had so much to offer.

It was my job to find innovative ways to make better use of that invaluable asset and the scant twenty hours of meeting time we had each year. That required educating the trustees so they could advise the hospital leadership on matters of strategy, quality of care, and financial performance. It also meant inspiring them with stories of heroic care delivery and innovation so the trustees could be passionate advocates of the hospital's work. How did I accomplish that goal? It all started with a focus on the hospital's mission. I optimized their precious time together by planning board meeting agendas a year at a time to make sure they addressed all four key components of the mission: patient care, research, education, and community health improvement. We also began the tradition of holding an annual retreat for trustees so they could more thoroughly examine different aspects of the health-care system and the hospital's mission to deepen the trustees' understanding and commitment. And we created subcommittees that gave board members opportunities to contribute their special expertise where it could have the greatest impact.

Isn't that what you want for yourself? To focus on what matters most and to spend your time and talent where it can make a meaningful difference? So, just like MGH and all great organizations, you need a clear statement of your purpose. If you are paralyzed by the idea of starting this process because of the enormity of this first step, take a deep breath. We will ease into it with surprisingly simple, even fun, exercises. Help is here for you at every turn.

What Is Your Personal Mission?

You may have noticed that I asked you what *your* mission is. It is important to start by thinking about what's most important to *you.* I am asking you to listen to your own voice. Not your parents' or your boss's or the neighbors', or the voice of the ever-popular "they" who always seem to have a lot to say about just about everything. Your plan will not be successful unless it reflects your most authentic passions and employs your own brand of genius.

When I first set out to write my own mission statement, I was surprised by how many voices I recalled telling me what I should do. My mother thought my talents for healing would lead me to a career in medicine. A former teacher thought my skill with puzzles and problem solving would make me a great engineer. It took a while to sort through all that input and think about what I loved doing and where I could make a unique contribution. Since physics was among my least favorite subjects in school, engineering was clearly *not* it. So, do take some time to consider the advice of others, and decide how well it fits. Your mission must be an authentic reflection of you or it will not serve its intended purpose.

Joy Notes

Feeling like we've spent our time well is essential to our happiness. We have opportunities every day to add to our reservoir of joy when we perform good acts or just connect meaningfully with others. When we are able to use our unique gifts to help someone or make something better, we feel like we're making a meaningful contribution and our lives matter. American psychologist Abraham Maslow showed in his famous hierarchy of needs that self-actualization is the highest driver of human motivation. According to his well-regarded theory, people who fulfill their potential experience moments of profound happiness and harmony. Furthermore, people must do what they are individually suited to do in order to be at peace with themselves.[3]

So, what talents and passions do you have that we can set on a (very friendly) collision course with the needs of others? When we were kids, we had no trouble tooting our horns or saying what we loved. We declared with glee what we wanted to be or do when we grew up and we never questioned whether we could do whatever we wanted. Have you ever heard a toddler say, "I want to be a fireman when I grow up, but I'm afraid I won't be good enough?" If your ability to declare your talents has been socialized out of you, you'll need to flex that muscle. And if you can't say off the top of your head what you love doing, you will have to work on that too. Let's start with a warm-up exercise that's fun and easy and can help you get back in touch with what makes your heart sing.

EXERCISE

Part One: Proud Accomplishment

Start by thinking of an accomplishment you're proud of, something that succeeded because of the unique blend of talents you provided. This could be anything. Maybe you pulled off a marketing coup, made a stellar presentation, or defused a volatile family situation. Perhaps you realized that some of the kids at your child's school didn't have coats and you organized a clothing drive. Or, it could be that you threw a killer salsa dance party that people still talk about years later.

Grab your notebook and start writing. What was it you did that makes you smile just to remember the experience? It should be comforting to know that there are no wrong answers here. One of the most valuable lessons I learned happened when I was helping our local National Public Radio affiliate with its strategic plan. At that time, John Davidow was the news director at WBUR and he said something that has stuck with me for years. He talked about how talented his reporters were and yet so different from one another. "If I gave the same story idea to five reporters, they would come back with five very different stories, all excellent. There are many good ways to tell a story." So, just get started writing and don't worry about getting it "right." Just tell your story. You can always come back to this exercise and add and edit as you see fit.

Part Two: What Made You So Successful?

There, that wasn't such heavy lifting, was it? Now that your muscles are warmed up, it's time to complete the second part of this exercise. Jot down in your notebook what it was about you that made you so successful. What combination of skills and abilities made you uniquely suited to pull it off?

Whatever the specifics of the accomplishment you chose, you're looking for a feeling of success and ease, the sense that you were the right person for the task because it called on your passions and talents so that you were naturally drawn to do it. These are the hallmarks of your calling.

Look a Little Deeper

Now that you're warmed up, it's time for some more self-reflection. Who *are* you? When is the last time you really looked at yourself: your skills, passions, and desires? What drives you? If you've been around any teenagers lately, chances are you've seen them hanging around in front of a mirror, playing with their hair, making funny faces, or trying out different voices. They spend a lot of time considering who they are and how they want to present themselves to others. But at some point, that self-examination stops and we get caught up in the busyness that keeps us from looking inside ourselves with any regularity.

This process of self-reflection often makes me think of my annual hiking trips through the national parks. Most of these parks have some pretty gorgeous scenery you can see from the car as you drive through them. And it's wonderful that so much beauty is accessible to anyone who makes the trip. It's always striking to me, however, that there's so much more splendor and adventure waiting for those who are willing to take the time and make the effort to explore what's beyond the surface. Sometimes it's scary to confront the power of nature and to find the energy for a big climb. But if you're willing to go inside and work a little harder than the average bear, you are usually rewarded with some spectacular views and peak experiences.

And so it is with our selves. It takes some effort to look at our innermost thoughts and desires. It can require some real courage if we're afraid of what we might see. Honest self-examination can indeed open up some new frontiers or require us to face some facts about ourselves that we'd just as soon ignore. Yet we turn a deaf ear to our inner voice at our peril. Failing to pay attention to what our hearts are trying to tell us can mean missing out on discovering what's really going to fulfill us.

What Is Holding You Back?

Fear is often at the root of what is holding us back from pursuing our deepest desires and getting what we really want. We're afraid that if we try, we might fail. Even though we know, on some level, that failure is guaranteed if we *don't* try, it somehow feels less risky not to put ourselves out there. It is often quite liberating when we face our fears head on. I've seen coaching clients and workshop participants address fears they'd been carrying with them for years and get past them in a matter of minutes once they were able to name the problem and make a plan.

Examine Your Self-Doubt

When I was a hospital senior vice president, Brenda came to interview for a job opening in one of my departments. She was a program coordinator who administered the complex logistics of a training program that was integrated with Harvard Medical School. It was clear from our discussion that she was able to manage lots of details, cope with some challenging personalities, and meet countless deadlines. So I asked her why she was interested in this administrative assistant position that was clearly less involved than what she was already doing and several pay grades below her current position. She said that what she really wanted was a management career and that "sometimes you need to take a step back in order to take a step forward." When I pointed out that this move would be a step *away* from reaching her goal, her face fell and her shoulders drooped. But something sparkled in Brenda and I was impressed by her talent and earnest desire to make a bigger contribution to the hospital. Something was holding her back and I wanted to help her figure out what that was and how to drive past that roadblock so she could get what she really wanted. I offered to mentor her through the steps necessary to become a manager. She gratefully accepted.

Brenda came to our first meeting eager to get on the path to becoming a manager. We started by reviewing her résumé with an eye toward identifying where she was relative to where she needed to be to land a job in management. The most glaring hole was readily apparent—she didn't have a college education. When I asked her why she never pursued the bachelor's degree that was essential for her to achieve her goal of becoming a manager, she told me that she was no good at math and there was no way she could make it through college. I asked her where she got that idea. She told me about her middle school math teacher who had humiliated her in front of her class and told her publicly that she had no aptitude for math. Hello? Within minutes, we had reached the source of the dilemma that had plagued her for decades. Shame on her math teacher who, thirty years earlier, had robbed a young girl of her confidence. But now we knew what we were dealing with and what was really holding her back.

Question Your Limiting Beliefs

I pointed out to Brenda that in order to be successful in her current job, she did math every day, some of it very sophisticated. So, when she turned to making her list of strengths, she could include math among them. Suddenly, all kinds of possibilities opened up for her. You will see her story unfold as you move through the rest of the steps in this book.

The Foundation of YOUR Mission

Let's go on with creating the building blocks for your mission statement. In this section, you will continue to look at your passions and talents. You will also look at your core values and the principles that will guide your way. Taken together, these elements will illuminate your purpose so that your mission statement can reflect who you are, what you intend to do, and why it is important. This statement should inspire you and ignite your commitment to fulfilling it.

It is now time to round out a description of your talents. If you find it hard to wax on about what you're really good at doing, it might help to think about how others see you. Who knows you best? What would they say are your greatest strengths?

EXERCISE

Talent Inventory

Here are some more questions to ask yourself to help you get started. Then, take it as far as you can go and record your findings in your notebook.

- What are my unique skills, talents, and strengths?
- What's my first instinct when approaching a new challenge?
- What is the first thing I do when I enter a room?[4]
- What do I spontaneously contribute to the activity of a group?
- What do I feel compelled to do for others?
- What are others seeking when they come to me for help?

To illustrate how this all works, let's look at Raymond, a fictional coaching client (who draws on aspects of a few real-life clients) with an innovative ear for music and a passion for blending harmonies. When he thought about his musical gifts in relation to these questions, Raymond realized that he had an unusual set of skills. He was one of those rare artists who had lots of left-brained analytic and organizational abilities to complement his considerable creative talents. He had a unique ability to interpret great works and to imagine how to blend the many orchestral instruments to create arrangements that had a visceral impact on the audience. His colleagues always looked to him to find the flourish that would add the necessary flair to elevate a piece from well executed to exceptionally moving.

Raymond's father, an aspiring concert pianist who never fulfilled his own ambitions, saw the creative genius his son possessed and was thrilled at the notion that someone in his family could rise to the heights he'd once imagined for himself. Raymond took his father's enthusiasm to heart and always assumed he'd become a pianist wowing crowds across the globe with his brilliant interpretations of classical compositions. He was excited to have so many talents on which to build an amazing musical career. He crafted a mission statement that really lit him up: "To beautify the world with musical harmonies that soothe the soul and ignite the spirit."

Often, what you are good at is highly correlated with what you enjoy doing. One of the reasons I'm so passionate about creating a personal strategic plan is that I want to make sure my life is full of the things that I love most. To do that, you need to know what those things are. As sad as it might sound, a lot of us just haven't given much thought to what lights us up from the inside. Here in your virtual Walden Woods, you have the perfect opportunity to pay close attention to what you enjoy most.

EXERCISE

Name Your Passions

What are you most passionate about? You can free-associate and write down anything that comes to mind. If you're stuck, here are a few provocative questions to get you going.

- What are some peak experiences I've enjoyed in my life?
- What activities am I naturally drawn to?
- What is my favorite kind of vacation?
- How do I spend my spare time?
- What are my hobbies?
- What do I do when I'm procrastinating?

It's about this time in the Business of Life workshops that a lot of light bulbs start going off. Remember Danielle, the disgruntled fashion buyer who was stuck by inertia in a job she hated? As she worked on these questions in the hushed room of the workshop she attended, she blurted out that she'd been working for more than twenty years and hadn't done a single thing she loved doing. At that moment, she resolved to make a major change. While inertia had her in a holding pattern with fear of letting go of the familiar, she saw that it was actually riskier to stay in a soul-sapping situation than to cut her losses and try something new. The cost of staying put and hating her life was too high. Especially now that she saw, on paper, that her love of cooking and the arts found no expression in her current life. While she couldn't yet see how it would, she knew that it must.

Doing What Comes Natur'lly

A wonderful benefit of creating a mission built on the foundation of your talents and passions is that you're likely to craft one that plays to your strengths and comes naturally to you. When that is the case, success comes with relative ease. Has anyone ever complimented you for doing something that comes so easily to you that you didn't even recognize it was a special talent? Did you respond by saying, "Oh, that was nothing, anyone can do that"? Well, not everyone can compose a symphony or twirl a baton while reciting poetry. If someone has indeed complimented you on one of your particular aptitudes, what is it that you can do that you thought anyone could do? Go back and put that on your list of talents.

I asked a client I'll call Thelma if I could interview her about how she applies what she learned in the Business of Life management course offered her by her employer a couple of years earlier. She had mentioned she used many of the tools in both her work and personal life since taking the class. I told her I was interested in her experience because she's one of the most strategic thinkers I know and she works so well with the planning framework in the workplace. As if to make my point for me, she said she was glad I saw those traits in her because they happen so instinctively, she wasn't even aware of them.

Have you ever seen a job description that seemed to be written for you, almost as though the person writing it knew you and wanted you to have the job? It's an amazing feeling to see the details of what you love listed as qualifications you miraculously possess. That is like the time a family friend won a college scholarship designated for a student of high academic achievement who played piano and excelled on the high school tennis team. Now there's a niche not many people could fill, but it played right into his quirky mix of gifts.

Core Values

The final building block of your mission embraces your core values. These are the principles you hold most dear that will guide your path toward fulfilling your mission. My daughter calls these her "words to live by."

What matters most to you? You need to think about that because what you value will illuminate your way, guide how you conduct yourself, and determine what you leave behind. Guiding principles serve as an excellent filter when setting priorities. For example, after all my struggles to have my second child, being fully present for my kids and showering them with love was my highest priority, along with keeping up with my many responsibilities in the executive suite at work. Achieving both objectives took laser-like focus, and using my guiding principles helped me make decisions that would keep my energies focused on what was truly most important to me.

What Are Core Values?

Core values reflect the underlying philosophy that determines how you want to conduct your business and life. Organizations frequently use their statement of core values to describe how they expect their employees to treat their colleagues and customers as they work to carry out their mission.

While I was the senior vice president for strategic planning at Massachusetts General Hospital, we updated the institution's mission statement to reflect the hospital's passionate commitment to patient-centered care as well as to improving the health of people in the surrounding communities. In this example, you can see how the hospital's dedication to excellence and quality combines with its core values of compassion, collaboration, and innovation to infuse the MGH's purpose of providing patient care, research, and education with passion and commitment.

MASSACHUSETTS GENERAL HOSPITAL'S REVISED MISSION STATEMENT

Guided by the needs of our patients and their families, we aim to deliver the very best health care in a safe, compassionate environment; to advance that care through innovative research and education; and to improve the health and well-being of the diverse communities we serve.

This revision replaced a far more utilitarian version:

To provide the highest quality care to individuals and to the local and distant communities we serve, to advance care through excellence in biomedical research, and to educate future academic and practice leaders of the health-care professions.

Can you feel the difference between these two statements? The earlier version espouses some important values such as quality and excellence. The revision built on that foundation, but made explicit the desire to place patients and families at the center of the mission and to bring safety and compassion into the mix. In this way, both the people who work at the hospital and those who use its services can see how vital they are to the hospital's purpose. We shared a draft of the revision with hundreds of employees, staff, and patients to get their responses. Hospital leadership settled on this version only after ensuring that it reflected their values and made them proud to be affiliated with this august institution.

Some Common Core Values

I have worked over the years with many organizations to articulate their core values. Here is a sample of some frequently cited guiding principles:

Accountability	Dedication	Honesty	Passion
Collaboration	Efficiency	Innovation	Quality
Commitment	Excellence	Integrity	Relationships
Compassion	Fun	Loyalty	Spirituality

It's hard to argue with any of these, but you will likely value some more than others, relatively speaking. And, of course, there are many other possibilities that may speak more directly to you. You will create your own list and it should reflect what matters most to *you*. It seems like mom and apple pie, but some people do lose sight of what truly matters and stray from their right path from time to time.

Live Your Values

Miranda looked for success in all the wrong places. Trying to impress others and please her parents, she set out to shatter the glass ceiling and to do whatever it took to make it to the corner office. And she did. The only problem is that she didn't really *want* to be there. She got so caught up in winning the game she had been playing for so long, she'd forgotten why she'd started playing it in the first place. Driven to win the approval of others, Miranda compromised her personal values so many times to climb the corporate ladder that she lost many friends and her sense of spirit along the way.

Looking back on it all in her late fifties, she realized in a rare moment of self-reflection that she'd sacrificed her soul to acquire all the outer trappings of success. She'd become the CEO of her large corporation, served on the boards of international companies, and sported a diamond the size of a skating rink. Yet despite the rewards and recognition, she was spiritually bankrupt. She hated just about everything to do with her job and looked at her cutthroat colleagues with suspicion and disdain. Sadly, she saw pretty much the same thing when she looked in the mirror. As Miranda imagined herself rocking on the porch swing in her twilight years, she saw herself surrounded by people whom she paid to take care of her. She saw herself feeling empty, alone, insecure, and unfulfilled. And despite her undeniable professional achievements, she still had the urgent sense that she wasn't good enough and never would be. She had lost herself in her quest to impress others. Worse, those people she had impressed didn't like her much and certainly wouldn't choose to spend their free time with her.

During her coaching sessions, Miranda discovered that she had been chasing external validation of her worth and had failed to look deep inside her own self to discover what truly mattered most to her. She finally understood that she would have to take responsibility for her actions by defining her personal values and adopting principles that would guide her future choices. She realized that she wanted to help new generations of women avoid the mistakes she had made that had taken such a toll on her and everyone who had been on the receiving end of her legendary bursts of anger. Later in this book, you will read more about Miranda's quest to put her considerable talents to use in a way that would empower young women to find career success. She learned to create meaningful, authentic relationships, both personal and professional, and experienced true joy for the first time that she could remember.

EXERCISE

Words to Live By

What ideology guides your actions? Think about the values and underlying philosophy that determine how you intend to live your life. These are your guiding principles. Record them in your notebook.

Putting It All Together

You've identified where your talents make you shine, where you feel most satisfied sharing them, and the issues, causes, people, and arenas that capture your passion. You've also zeroed in on the guiding principles you'll use as a compass. Hopefully, as you look at these elements together, you see your mission coming into focus and are ready to capture that clarity in a mission statement. As you prepare to write your statement, I offer some final questions to help you integrate what you've listed in the previous exercises into a statement of your purpose.

EXERCISE

Part One: Answer these Guiding Questions

- What would you want people to say about you at your funeral? Or maybe you'll find it less morbid to imagine people holding a "lifetime achievement" dinner in your honor. What are they saying about you? Your accomplishments? How you lived out your purpose? What are they saying was your unique contribution to the world? What would you say if you could write your own obituary (way, way in the future, of course)?
- If you didn't have to earn a living, how would you spend your time?
- If you had a million dollars to donate, what cause would you support?
- What would you do if you knew you couldn't fail?

Record your answers in your notebook.

Part Two: Write Your Mission Statement

This is a declaration of your life's purpose—why you are here. Craft your mission statement as if you couldn't fail. Think big and be aspirational. Don't worry that your mission seems too big or grandiose. Just write down what feels right. You are taking this one step at a time. Following this exercise are some frequently asked questions and sample mission statements for you to review now or after you take a first stab at your mission statement.

Frequently Asked Questions

At this point in the process, many people have questions about how to produce an effective mission statement. Here are some of the most common queries I've received.

• *What is a good mission statement and how is it written?* An effective mission statement describes your primary purpose in a way that inspires you to take values-based action to fulfill it. It serves as a filter to help you focus your actions in accordance with your intention. Use language that motivates you and is clear and memorable.

• *How long should my mission statement be?* I'm often asked about the "right" length for a mission statement. Some say it needs to pass the coffee mug test, meaning it should be short enough for you to look at as you sip your daily cup of joe. In truth, the length needs to be what's right for you, and you are the only one who can determine that. If it motivates and inspires you, it's right. It's often helpful to keep it short enough so you can remember and recite it easily. A passing glance at a framed version should energize and inspire you.

• *Will you share some sample mission statements?* I used to share my own personal mission statement in my workshops as an example of what one looks like, but stopped doing that because people would sometimes make a Mad Libs version of mine and call it their own. I will share examples from previous workshop participants to show you some effective statements. You will see mine later on, but please do create yours before you read it.

Sample Mission Statements

Use the following examples as models for crafting your mission statement, but please avoid the temptation to make a few edits to someone else's statement and call it a day.

Personal Mission Statements

With thanks to the talented managers who took my leadership development course at MGH and gave me permission to share their personal missions, here are several examples of well-crafted mission statements.

- "To achieve personal and professional success by utilizing my knowledge and skill set when and wherever possible. I will also strive to help others and give back to the community in every way that I know how."
- "To operate from a balanced mental, physical, and spiritual center while sharing my creative talents in both my professional and personal life."
- "Through my compassion and generosity, I will set the best practice for my philanthropic endeavors and will inspire others to do the same. I will fulfill the need for humane education: teaching others the principles of kindness, compassion, and respect for all life."
- "My personal mission is to be a great mom, a true and faithful partner to my husband, a good citizen, a caring daughter, daughter-in-law, and family member as well as a good friend. With my husband, we will raise smart, happy, good and independent children who will grow up to be productive and successful adults. I will have fun at the same time as accomplishing these goals. I also want to be faithful to God and want to help others in their time of need by donating time, talents, and money whenever possible."

- "To strive to achieve consistent growth and education in my professional career, in conjunction with a harmonious family life."
- "My personal mission is to value myself first, so that I can give more to others with a clear mind and open heart. I will rely on my humor and empathy to help others when they need it and give to those who need it most."
- "To provide compassionate care for less fortunate and needy throughout the local community and the entire world."
- "I am an adoring mother driven by passion for my children, husband, and family. I strive to support, motivate, and bring joy to those I encounter throughout my life. My life is enriched and rounded out with family, friends, career, volunteer service, spirituality, and my adorable dog, who always makes me smile."

Organizational Mission Statement

Remember Peggy and Gail, the cancer survivors who wanted to start a program for kids? Here's their organization's mission statement.

OUR SPACE, INC. MISSION

The mission of Our Space is to embrace children and teens who have faced or are confronting cancer. Our Space will inspire peace, spirit, and healing within a supportive community, through play, learning, and creative exploration.

My Own Mission Statements

I had occasion to use my own personal mission statement to help me make an important decision very recently. While writing this book, I was confronted with a choice. My son was preparing for his bar

mitzvah, an important rite of passage for Jewish boys on their thir-
teenth birthday. As part of this ceremony, which marks a young man's
entry into manhood, he needed to lead a large portion of the service
as well as write and deliver a commentary. This required work of epic
proportions and not a small amount of his mother's attention to teach
him the skills he'd need to excel. As the date neared, it became clear to
me that I could not keep up with my consulting obligations, help my
son prepare fully, and devote the intense focus necessary to write my
book all at the same time. Something had to give, and the book was
the only thing that had any give in the short term. Facing the prospect of falling three weeks behind on my writing schedule (remember,
you're dealing with a planner here; procrastination is painful for me),
I needed centering to make a clear decision and allow myself to fully
commit to whatever I chose to do. So, I turned to my personal mission
statement:

> Devoted to delighting my family, friends, clients, colleagues, and
> community, I strive to laugh loudly, love deeply, and nourish all
> with food for thought and balm for the soul. To use my unique
> talents fully to inspire others to connect with their passions and
> fulfill their potential so together we shine our light, spread joy,
> and leave the world a better place for having lived here—with
> purpose.

In an instant, I knew that putting my book aside for those three
weeks was what I needed to do. Concentrating my efforts to help my
son fill his potential at this critical juncture was central to my personal mission. I picked up the phone and told my husband what I'd
discovered and prepared him for the fact that I'd be "going underground" after the bar mitzvah to spend some intensive time writing
to get the book back on schedule. With Plan B firmly in place, I was
able to put my attention where it was needed. And when my son delivered the performance of a lifetime and basked in the pride of know-

ing he'd done his very best, there was no doubt I had made the right decision.

Following my personal mission in no way meant compromising my professional ideals, but I want to emphasize that while critically important to me, my career is only one aspect of my life's mission. My work and business has its own mission:

> To guide individuals and organizations in identifying their unique talents, passions, and purpose and to provide the tools necessary to harness this power to ensure the joyful fulfillment of their individual and collective missions and, in so doing, improve the world.

You will notice that the two statements complement one another and work in harmony. But a balanced life is about much more than work alone, so that is reflected by the fact that I have more than one statement. My associates and I are all well aware of the company's mission statement and it guides all of our decision making relative to business matters. Likewise, many families have a family mission statement that helps members of that important operating unit get on the same page and operate in solidarity.

Take one last look at your mission statement (of course, you can go back and revise it whenever you like) and put some final flourishes on it if you are so moved. Record your mission statement, guiding principles, and the most essential insights from your self-assessment on the left side of your Custom Life Closet for easy reference. You may even wish to make an attractive printout of your mission and hang it where you can see it every day to be reminded of what matters most to you. You may also want to consider writing another mission statement for any aspect of your life that seems to call out for its own. Most essentially, use your mission statement(s) to remind yourself of what brings you joy and matters most.

Toolbox

Breath

Accessible to anyone at any time, focused breathing is a tool you can use to center yourself and get clarity as you contemplate your mission or at any point in the planning process. Whether you call focusing on your breath for a few moments meditation or just taking a breather, take regular moments to jump off the treadmill to reclaim your focus. Taking time to just be quiet and listen to what your inner voice has to say to you is a critical step in finding your metaphorical song so you bring your beautiful music to life.

Step ❷

Vision: Imagine the Sweet Smell
(Sound, Look, and Feel) of Success

"If you don't know where you are going, any road will get you there."[1]
—Lewis Carroll

Congratulations. You have named your life's mission and you *are* going to put your talents to work to meet a need in the world. So how do you begin to do that? By stepping into the future and imagining that it's already done.

Creating a vision statement is step two of building your strategic plan. You will paint a vivid verbal picture of what life looks like when you are using your gifts fully, doing what you love most, and accomplishing what you set out to do. Your vision statement describes the point on the map you want to reach. While it won't tell you how you'll get there, it serves as your inspiration and the foundation for your business planning. You can't figure out what stands between where you are and where you want to be and how you'll travel the distance until you can clearly see your destination. It's your personal definition of success.

But in the Business of Life, your vision is more than just the X that marks the spot labeled "I've arrived." It's also a description of the journey—the life you'll savor along the way. Think of yourself as a skier standing at the trail map on the mountain. Your task is to choose the path that matches your ability, passions, and resources. Maybe you have a natural gift for skiing, love the exhilaration of flying down the mountain, and have a great pair of high-performance skis.

You might choose the double black diamond slope, with its bumps and adrenaline-pumping jumps. Or perhaps you're more laid back and would prefer a contemplative cross-country meander through the valley to the waterfall.

Your vision statement will capture all of this: the endpoint—where you're enjoying the fruits of doing what you set out to do—as well as the path and cadence that bring you pleasure as you head in that direction. In this chapter, you will complete a series of exercises that will define the elements of your vision. By the end of this phase, you will put them all together in a comprehensive picture so you can create the steps that will take you toward this satisfying future.

Visioning may sound a bit ethereal if you're a left-brain analytic person, but it's absolutely pragmatic. These compelling images will motivate you and keep you energized and moving forward productively. Whether you are creating a plan for a project at work, making more space for your family and hobbies, or taking on your whole life's mission, your vision statement puts a picture of what you are trying to achieve in your mind's eye and gives you a target to shoot for. It also reminds you very clearly of why hitting that target is worth it.

Bill is an architect who has run his own successful firm for decades. As the president of a million-dollar-plus nonprofit organization, he asked me to guide the board of trustees through a strategic planning process. After working on the mission statement, he was eager to jump right to setting strategies for achieving it. That's step five and, like a lot of people, he wanted to cut out the "softer" preliminaries and just get right to it. So it was gratifying to see the light bulb go on over his head as I explained the importance of creating a vision statement. He exclaimed, "Oh, I see now. If we can say more clearly what we want, we can figure out which strategies are most likely to get us there." As simple as this sounds, it was a revelation to him.

Interestingly, as an architect, Bill used visioning quite naturally with his clients by asking them how they wanted to use the space they had engaged him to design and what they wanted to accomplish there. Furthermore, he recognized that the other trustees who worked in a variety of industries needed a common understanding of the organization's aspirations and that taking time at the outset to sharpen that vision would avoid time-stealing disagreements later in the process.

If you are leading a group at work, think about your people rowing toward a goal. Imagine what would happen if one person was headed in another direction. At best, he would slow the team's progress and at worst he would get your boat spinning in circles, making everyone seasick in the process.

And so it is for you. When a vision statement does its job, it's so vivid that you can easily see yourself in the new reality you would like to create. And it will get all parts of you working in harmony; your heart *and* head will be rowing in the same direction so you don't spin from inner conflict. If you're clear on where you're headed, it's much easier to see what it will take to accomplish your goals. And because it requires thinking about all the things you need to enjoy your life, creating your vision statement is actually fun and inspiring.

Having a Wonderful Time, Wish You Were Here

Think of your vision statement as a postcard from the future. You imagine yourself at a point a year or five or ten years down the line where you are happy and fulfilled. As you put yourself firmly in this picture, you use all of your senses to fully experience this vision— what true success would be like for you. Are you running a new business? Serving a needy population with an entrepreneurial nonprofit organization? Are you sitting in a beautifully decorated office? Cutting the ribbon for a new school you've helped open? Are you thriving at your demanding job, but this time making room for all the other things that mean so much to you, such as running outside with the dog or going out for real romance with your spouse? What are you seeing, smelling, hearing, feeling? Who is with you? You're on vacation? Are you trekking through the mountains in Nepal or lounging in a hammock with a good book? Take time to note all the elements that surround the future you, and imagine this delicious scene in all its glory, with you at the center.

Many Western definitions of success focus on achieving a goal such as reaching a career milestone and crossing it off the list, but a well-lived life includes so much more. The soul-satisfying activities that make you feel whole belong in your vision, too. Interestingly, as you'll see throughout this book, bringing more *you* to your life can increase your effectiveness at work exponentially.

Life is serious business, but who said the ride shouldn't be fun? It isn't just about achieving results; it's about creating warm relationships, giving of yourself, and feeling joy and pleasure. In fact, a happy and fulfilled you is one of the greatest gifts you can give to the world. So, let's get started creating the building blocks of your vision statement.

EXERCISE

Postcard from the Future

I invite you to have some fun fantasizing about what a perfect day looks like for you. Sit comfortably with your notebook or computer. Put your mission statement firmly in your mind. Close your eyes for a few moments and picture yourself at some point in the future, fully living your dream and fulfilling your purpose. Breathe deeply and engage all of your senses. Describe what you experience as you imagine moving through your day. As you write it all down, be sure to state everything in the present tense and keep it positive. You experience what you put your attention on, so focus on pleasant images and describe what you see as though it were happening right now.

- What are you doing?
- Where are you?
- What does the space look like? Are you indoors or outside? Is it sunny and warm or are you in a dark room filled with technol-

ogy? What colors do you see? Is every room filled with fresh flowers? Are there whiteboards on the walls?

- Who is with you? Are you working in blissful solitude or surrounded by an unruly bunch of creative types? How are you relating to one another?
- Are you working in peace and quiet or is there music playing in the background?
- What do you need to have to make every day a joyful pleasure? The chance to connect deeply with other people? A fix of chocolate? Lots of laughter?
- What must you avoid to be happy? Do you hate conflict? Barking dogs? Traffic?

Write down anything that comes to you in your notebook and just start a stream-of-consciousness brain download. Answer all the questions above and anything else that comes to you. You will add to your "postcard" as you work your way through the following sections and you'll refine your vision in the final exercise.

Mission + You = Vision

In case you are feeling any pressure about getting your vision statement "right," let me assure you this task is eminently doable and virtually impossible to get wrong. That's because it's all about *you*, and you're the owner/operator of that fine operation.

One of the most important factors that separates inspired leaders from the sea of competent managers is a clear vision. It's hard to persuade other people to contribute to your success if you can't tell them what you want. And now that you are running the business of your life, it's time you get clear on what *You, Inc.* is going to produce. No one knows you better than you, so there is no one more qualified to define success on your terms.

You used your talent inventory in the last chapter to help define your mission, and it may be quite similar to other people's statements.

A lot of people and organizations have missions that overlap, or even sound nearly identical. But the visions they have for fulfilling those missions can be quite different, because each is built on the visioner's guiding principles and unique skills, experiences, and passions.

How you choose to carry out a given mission is a reflection of who you are: your own skills, likes, values, and quirky sense of what's fun or fulfilling. You're looking for the path that's a perfect fit for your talents, something that excites you and feels easy because it lets you do what comes naturally to you.

Say you identified feeding the hungry as your life's mission. The task of nourishing the world is enormous, and there are endless possible visions for accomplishing it. A right-brain, creative type might take on this mission by creating delicious new recipes for food that is stable without refrigeration and can easily be shipped and stored in areas without electricity. An analytical left-brain thinker might be intrigued by the logistics of creating a distribution system that delivers her creative friend's innovative cuisine to hungry people in remote third world villages. Yet another person with the very same mission might enjoy solving the puzzle of how to get around corrupt governments and bandits who siphon off the aid being offered by relief groups to the souls whose survival depends it.

Each of these people is working toward a common purpose, and all make an essential contribution in their own way.

EXERCISE

Pack It with Passion

To infuse your vision with passion and fun, go back to the lists of your talents and interests that you made in step one. How many of your passions can you pack in as you carry out your mission? Love problem solving? How can you bring your sleuthing skills into the picture? Would people laugh with recognition to see you, a dog lover, as a detective in the canine unit? Put that possibility on the table. What else makes you smile? You'll want your vision to be sprinkled with those feel-good spices.

The Magic Word for a Powerful Vision: AGLOW

"Neither do men light a candle, and put it under a bushel, but on a candlestick: and it gives its light unto all that are in the house."

— Jesus of Nazareth

Your vision statement isn't something you'll write and file away. You'll refer to it often, even daily, so it should be inspirational. Create an image that propels you forward, compelling you to pursue goals that will move you along your path. It should light you up from the inside with a glow that radiates to everyone around you. Just reading it should energize you.

You can ensure that your vision statement has the power to set you AGLOW by making it:

Authentic
Grand
Laudable
Optimistic
Wondrous

EXERCISE

Get Glowing

Grab your notebook and record your thoughts as we drill down into each of these elements. The insights, images, and desires that surface as you go along may become the pearls that you string together to create a complete vision.

1. Make it authentic: First and foremost, your vision must allow you to be true to who you really are, not someone else's vision of what they'd like you to be. What do you most value? What are the gifts that only you can share with the world? That must be expressed in your vision statement. You will not heed your calling if you are trying to be a pale imitation of someone else. You need to focus your energies on being the best YOU possible. As motivational speaker Mike Robbins says in his book of the same name, "Be yourself. Everyone else is already taken."[2]

I can't stress enough the importance of authenticity in writing your vision. Make it reflect your genuine dreams and desires. You've put a lot of effort into finding your personal genius and thinking about how to put that to work in service of the world. Stay focused there. Dig deep.

2. Make it grand: This is the time to think big, audacious thoughts. One of my students told me that his grandfather used to say, "Shoot for the sky and you might hit the top of the coconut tree. Shoot for the tree and you may hit the ground." Take his advice and aim high. Writing a vision statement is about defining your ideal, not what you think may be possible. This is *not* the time to limit your thinking and cut off your options because you believe your fantasy is too big, too bold, or too anything ever to come true. We will test those limiting beliefs later. You may be quite surprised to see what's feasible once you have a vivid vision of where you're headed and you're armed with the information and tools presented in the upcoming chapters. So, suspend disbelief for now and think big.

If you knew you couldn't fail, what would you include in your picture of your perfect future? Would you be hanging out with rock stars? Write it down. Selling your artwork in high-end art galleries? Record that. Your fantasies need a place to live. For now, that will be in your notebook. Later, who knows? One thing is for sure. If you cross your dreams off your list, they won't come true. At least give them a shot.

3. Make it laudable: Since your mission is about using your talents to meet a need in the world, your vision should describe how your little corner of the world will be better because of the work your mission has set in motion. This doesn't mean you have to be Mother Teresa. A personal shopper who helps people find flattering styles that make them feel attractive and confident is providing a helpful service. You can be helpful without being perfect. What does the world need that you have to offer? Which population do you want to serve? Animals? Do you want to be a veterinarian, a conservationist who saves endangered species in the jungles of Africa, or a dog walker? Do you want to raise happy children and send them into the world? Help the hungry and homeless? Heal the sick? Tell killer jokes and relieve the stress of overwrought executives? Write it down.

4. Make it optimistic: This is essential. To be effective, your vision statement should describe your life in positive, present tense language as though you were already living your ideal. The whole point of creating a vision is to help you picture what you are trying to achieve so you can focus your efforts on filling in the colors in your paint-by-numbers future.

When you were a kid, what got you excited? Write that down. Your younger self may well have a lot to teach you. So put yourself in your size four Keds and try to remember: What did you want to be when you grew up? Think about how you would have answered that question at several points in your childhood. The answers may give you additional clues about your gifts and passions. You may no longer want to fight fires, but when you ask your younger self why he wanted to do that, he may tell you that he likes helping people and the excitement that comes with the urgency of a crisis. Not to mention, he'd get to drive really cool trucks and slide down a pole in the middle of the night.

Do those things still float your boat? You may want to look for activities that include them and make them part of your vision. How can you get that adrenaline rush while helping people? Or was it the shiny brass pole that caught your imagination? I hear pole-dancing classes are popping up in health clubs across the country.

5. Make it wondrous: Your vision should leave you in a state of "pinch me" wonder, where you are thrilled to look around at a life that includes everything you value and that rewards you for giving exactly what you're here to offer. The more you paint a picture with all the shades that inspire and energize you, the more committed you will be to breathing life into it. And commitment is what we want. Your mission depends on it.

Pull It Together

Take a moment to review this section and make sure you've recorded all of the elements that will make your future glow.

Igniting Your Glow May Feel Undoable, but Try It Anyway

Bruce and his wife, Mara, were thrilled that their careers were going so well, and they were proud of their two beautiful children. Yes, they'd hoped for three, but other than that, they couldn't quite figure out why their jobs and kids weren't enough to make them happy. With this vague sense of dissatisfaction, Bruce, a mid-level manager (ironically enough, a strategic planner) took one of my Business of Life courses. Besides learning some concrete business skills he could use on the job, Bruce was hoping to get to the bottom of his discontent and to develop a plan to bring more joy into his life to match the success he seemed to have on paper.

Bruce's personal mission was "to create a harmonious home life, raise happy, healthy, and productive children, and make a positive difference with my professional and volunteer work." That statement reflected who he was, but it gave him no clues about what was missing, so he was excited by the idea of imagining his perfect day and conjuring up the details of what he needed in his life for it to feel fun, fulfilling, and meaningful.

He nodded when I told his group to consider what would make them the happiest, rather than focusing on what wasn't working in their lives. As a strategist, he knew well that working toward a positive vision is much more productive than dwelling on shortcomings. It was pretty easy for him to come up with this vision statement:

BRUCE'S VISION STATEMENT

It is five years from now and our household is a crazy, mixed-up bastion of creative, controlled chaos. Our three little girls, ages three, six, and eight, are growing, giggling, and thriving at their preschool and public schools. They enjoy their friends and each other. Each girl has her own distinct personality, but they share our family's common values and there is always love and compassion present, even during their disagreements. I enjoy being their personal riding toy and delight in showering them with love, wisdom, and thousands of kisses.

My wife and I have reclaimed some of the time we had devoted to establishing our careers and made a commitment to a weekly date where we can focus on our love for each other and remember to laugh together. Every Saturday night, we get dressed up, go out for dinner, and do something that reminds us of why we fell in love so many years ago. Fun is a requirement. We remember to be silly with each other, not just with the kids. I remember, weekly, to look deeply into Mara's eyes and really see her. This fuels me and allows me to keep a sense of humor about all the times my kids' demands pull me away from my work. Because it reminds me that raising happy, productive children *is* my work, and this memory makes me smile and relax.

Just writing his vision down made Bruce smile and relax. He had a big *aha* moment when he put his finger on what had been making him dissatisfied in his otherwise pretty great life: he'd gotten into a groove so deep it was more like a rut. He and Mara had been having what could best be described as an "administrative relationship." Their brief time together each day was spent figuring out the family's complicated logistics and assigning chores. They'd stopped expressing their real love for each other, let alone having fun together. This became immediately apparent to Bruce as he envisioned his ideal life. And when he mentioned it to Mara, she nodded with recognition and pledged immediately to join him in making some changes.

Bruce's shiny vision ultimately transformed their lives, but committing it to paper was a struggle for him. He hesitated to write down what he longed for because there seemed to be no way he and Mara could have a third child and keep it all together—not with *their* schedules.

When I saw his brow furrow while he was writing his vision statement in class, I walked over and asked if he needed help. He said that his vision seemed impossible and he was trying to figure out a vision that was feasible, so I reminded him not to edit down his dreams. We're going for grand, optimistic, and wondrous, after all, and that means coming up with a picture of the ideal, not simply what's practical. A vision statement helps you figure out *what* you want. The work that follows in a strategic plan is about figuring out *how* to get it, even when it seems wildly impractical.

Bruce took a deep breath and went determinedly (if a bit skeptically) back to his writing. We'll meet up with him later in this book to see how he dealt with the nuts and bolts of living out his vision. For now, all I will say is that he figured out a lot of stuff—and lit his wife's light in the process. He even improved his work life. And it all started with stretching his imagination and expanding his notion of what was possible.

Toolbox

Suspend Disbelief

You are going to learn some skills and techniques later in this book that may well give you the tools to accomplish what now seems completely out of the question. So before you discount any dream or desire as unattainable, put your doubts aside and, for now, continue with the assumption that anything is possible.

Feel the Pull

Just as a magnet draws metal effortlessly toward it, an effective vision statement pulls you toward its fulfillment. There's something irresistible to your mind and heart about imagining yourself enjoying your life while you are using your native talents to do great things. Who wouldn't be lured by such a force? And, when you layer on those things that make your hours joyful, you look forward to the process of arriving at your vision.

As I wrote this book—a project with the simple, utilitarian mission: Complete Writing the Book—I was pulled along by a vision that had me sitting in my beautiful office with soothing, cheerful colors, a cup of tea, music playing, and my lush garden on view through the window. Because my vision had spelled out not only my larger goals for the book but also what would make my journey the most satisfying, I made sure that I had all the little touches in my office that made me glad to be there. The space was clean and peaceful. I enjoyed a lovely solitude when it was needed and made plans to be with cherished friends and family later, so I was alone, but not lonely. My kids knew they could pop in for a kiss or a question, but not linger. So, I was productive, but not isolated. In short, my office was someplace I wanted to be and, as a result, it wasn't a struggle to get my butt in the chair and get down to work on this enormous undertaking.

The hard work of writing was sweetened immeasurably by the grace notes I strung through my vision. And I read the comments of people whose lives had been changed for the better after taking my workshops. The image of readers lighting up as they figure out what they want and discovering a path to make it happen kept me going, knowing I was fulfilling an important mission.

Did my vision "attract" the experience it described? Well, what you think about, you bring about, as the saying goes. We also tend to act on impulses that arise from what we focus on. We visualize writing in a serene space, and soon comes the impulse to clear and paint the room, set up the desk, put down the first few sentences. And in that way, we move toward creating that new reality.

You will do things randomly if you haven't consciously chosen a direction, so crafting a vision statement means taking active control of your thoughts, focusing them on creating a deliberate reality that is fulfilling and provides lasting value.

Remember Raymond, the imaginary musician from the last chapter whose mission was to become a concert pianist? He had a remarkable gift for blending notes and melodies to interpret great works in astonishing ways that still respected the compositions' integrity. Further, he found that his gift compelled him to create new musical pieces that stretched the music-loving public's imagination.

Now, as he closes his eyes and imagines his happy future, he sees himself surrounded by other musicians. He is listening, enraptured, to a harmonic blend of orchestral instruments sending their sweet sounds through the air of a great theater, and he is thrilled to contribute to the symphony. While he is there, he feels the joy that comes with living this reality.

When he wakes from his reverie and finishes writing down his vision, he realizes that it's been a mighty long time since he's actually played the piano. He's so excited to get started, he immediately picks up the phone to call the maestro from his local symphony hall to find the name of a piano teacher who can help him hone his skills until he is an accomplished enough performer to flourish as a soloist. He's on his way to leading the life he's dreamed of.

Vision has an amazing way of giving birth to action.

EXERCISE

Joy Notes

Because you'll want to be sure that your vision is full of elements, large and small, that give you pleasure, spend some time taking note of just what those things are. I often suggest that my students carry a notebook for a day, even a week, and jot down the things they enjoy. Puzzles? A walk across the park on the way home? A bounding yellow lab puppy jumping on you as you walk in the door? If it makes you happy, write it down, and be sure there's room for it in your vision.

Finding Focus

I've seen many people make changes, large and small, based solely on the power of their mission and vision statements, together with their guiding principles.

Take Sandra, for example. She's the compassionate, ambitious professional we met in the last section whose mission statement described the way she wanted to "support, motivate, and bring joy to those I encounter throughout my life."

She'd been tested, strengthened, and ultimately inspired by a long struggle with infertility, and when she sat down to write her vision statement, she reached back to that experience and confirmed for herself that helping others with that issue would be an important part of her future. She'd been thinking about starting a nonprofit organization, and because that dream seemed grand and a bit daunting, she set her vision five years in the future:

SANDRA'S PERSONAL VISION STATEMENT

I have a loving husband and two happy children who are self-confident and aware of themselves. We laugh and love together every day.

I am instrumental in developing and leading the inpatient and outpatient Diabetes Wellness Center at my hospital. I grew this center from its nascent stages to the award-winning center it is today.

I am the cofounder of Fertility Within Reach, a successful nonprofit organization aimed at helping individuals who are impacted by the disease of infertility become their own best advocates for change. I personally advocate for insurance coverage of infertility services nationwide. As a result of these efforts, individuals gain the confidence they need to navigate the struggles of infertility, and thousands of babies are born to couples faced with the challenge of infertility.

I enjoy my vast network of friends, each of whom brings me something different. We laugh together, support each other, and help each other grow.

Sandra came to the Business of Life class because she had an ambitious agenda and needed a set of tools to manage everything she wanted to do at home, at work, and in her community. With so much fire in her belly, she ran the risk of burning herself out if she tried to do too much. And like a lot of capable people who can handle many things well, she faced the very real possibility that she'd expertly execute the wrong things—initiatives that didn't mean much to her. That could bring her external rewards, but not genuine success.

Her vision statement helped her keep her passions front and center, and laid the groundwork for setting some short- and long-term goals. Just one year later—not five, as she'd expected—she's gotten Fertility Within Reach off the ground. The project took off as she discovered the power of concentrating her abundant energy on her own passions. And the joy that infused her vision is now part of her everyday life.

Later, you'll see the shifts Sandra made, and the new habits that took shape, as she began setting priorities based on her vision.

Use Your Vision to Make Decisions

Perhaps you are considering making a big change. Your vision statement can give you some objectivity in moments of doubt. As I contemplated what it would mean for me to leave my senior position in one of the world's most prestigious institutions to work on my own without a safety net, I looked to the vision statement I'd written years earlier. To my great surprise, the words "Massachusetts General Hospital" did not even appear in the document. So, while I likened my departure from MGH after sixteen years of devoted service to bungee jumping, my vision statement confirmed that this leap was worth making.

MY PERSONAL VISION STATEMENT

Every day is productive and filled with joy and laughter. I feel happily connected to others and my life's purpose at all times. My time is spent with people I love, respect, and enjoy. I have enough time to myself, but never feel alone or lonely. I feel guided and protected, safe to explore all aspects of who I am and to express my being fully.

My family is thriving. Indeed, all of my relationships are harmonious, loving, and mutually beneficial. My children are healthy, happy, and fulfilled. They enjoy a strong sense of self and their place in the world. We remain deeply connected while they enjoy their independence. They are fine human beings with wonderful values and are contributing their special gifts to benefit the world. My husband and I continue to grow together while also pursuing our individual interests. We nurture and support one another and have a lot of fun. We are learning what we need to know about each other and we enjoy and appreciate being together. Our connection continues to deepen and grow.

My work is another way to fulfill my sense of purpose. I lead a team of talented people with great integrity, commitment, and good humor. Our work is devoted to helping, empowering, and healing others and reflects back on us daily. I have enough flexibility to balance work with family life and the pursuit of my other personal interests. I consistently feel deeply satisfied with my work and can see tangible benefits of my contributions.

I have ample time to enjoy nature. My life is structured to allow for lots of hikes and other ways to enjoy the outdoors with friends and family or in solitude. It is easy to "get away from it all" whenever the need arises. I am surrounded by beauty: in my home and work environments, on the faces of the people I see, radiating from my own heart.

My life has a profound positive impact on all it touches. I am rewarded enough financially to support myself and my family and to contribute significantly to worthy causes. My future is secure. I may retire comfortably whenever I am ready. My needs, both material and emotional, are modest and easily met. All of this joy and bounty flows easily to and through me. I enjoy good health and vitality, easily maintaining my fitness level and a healthy, comfortable weight. I have more than enough energy to accomplish anything I choose to do. I enjoy inner peace and have learned to accept myself with love, unconditionally.

I have found the balance of work and other pursuits that works for my family, friends, colleagues, clients, and community. I am fully present at all times and true to myself. The people in my life know, honor, respect, and support me and the choices that I've made. We all live together in joy, good health, and harmony.

This statement reflects my aspirations and serves as a daily reminder to make decisions that support living in the manner this vision describes. In many ways, my vision statement is a great affirmation that I'm already acting in accordance with my values and that much of what's written here is part of my reality. That's worth appreciating, and I most certainly do. It's also there to pull me back on track when I stray from some of my own principles. You may have noticed that I speak of ease in my statement because, as a driven achiever, it's good to be reminded that I could lighten up from time to time. That reminder truly does help me make more mindful decisions that continuously nudge me in the right direction.

Evaluate an Opportunity

Your vision statement can help with all kinds of decisions. A new opportunity presents itself. Should you take it? A quick look at your vision statement will help you decide whether doing so will contribute to your idea of success or whether it will take you in some random, aimless direction.

Say you're offered a job as a financial analyst. It sounds like an interesting challenge, and it's a promotion. You're momentarily intrigued. Then you look at your vision statement and realize your mission to become manager is going to require that you get some experience supervising people. The only thing you'll be supervising as an analyst is a bunch of spreadsheets. The new job would move you up all right, but in a direction that moves you away from your goal, not toward it. No, this isn't the best strategic move you can make. But it's a useful wake-up call. You are due for a promotion and resolve to make an appointment today to talk to your boss about giving you a project with a few people to manage.

Should I Say Yes or No?

Your vision can also be a useful filter for deciding what to add to your already overflowing plate. Does serving on that fundraising committee at your church contribute to your vision of the perfect day, month, or life? It's a good fit for a vision that says: "I am happily engaged with other people in all my pursuits; I am very active in my community." Serving on this committee will give you time to spend with people you like and respect while contributing to your church, which is very important to your life and the fabric of the community. So, it's a big YES; you're happy to serve.

Or your experience may be more like that of my coaching client Brandon, a busy executive juggling family and a career. His vision of a balanced life showed him thriving at work yet being available to attend his children's soccer games and concerts without drawing the disapproving glares of his colleagues.

When he was asked to join the board of directors of a prestigious company, he was flattered, and his first instinct was to say yes and enjoy hobnobbing with other high-powered businesspeople. However, when he asked for more details, he learned that there would be at least an additional fifteen to twenty hours of work per month involved, and that the board meetings were held in the evenings, making it difficult to free himself for those important events at his kids' school. So, with disappointment but not regret, he turned down the offer with the confidence that another opportunity would arise when his kids were older and his priorities shifted.

You can use your vision statement to make less momentous decisions, as well. For instance, is an intriguing invitation a distraction or a pleasant diversion? Imagine that a friend invites you to come for a weekend at her house by the seashore. You love the beach, and spending time by the water is part of your vision. But you're on deadline with a project and worry you can't fit it in. Your spirits sink at the idea of missing all the fun, so remembering your vision, you tell your friend about your dilemma, instead of automatically saying no. She surprises you by suggesting that you take the bedroom in the back of the house where you can work in peace. Now you can go to the beach for a couple of hours, go back and work with intense focus during peak sun hours, and join up with your pals for a nice dinner out. Sounds splendid, and it will actually help you be efficient and meet your deadline. You start packing.

Vision at Work: Tapping Into Passion

There's another benefit to having a juicy vision: that inspiring image is a great way to get others on board and supporting you in whatever you want to do.

I recently chaired the search committee for a rabbi of a good-sized synagogue. We had just completed a strategic plan for the congregation so we were clear about the kind of spiritual leader we wanted to recruit. We were told there was a shortage of rabbis nationally and that we'd be lucky to get a dozen candidates. Astonishingly, more than forty rabbis applied for the position. When we asked the candidates what attracted them to the job, they all cited the same thing: the vision statement described such an exciting future, they wanted to be a part of making it happen.

Whether you're leading a team in your workplace, on a football field, or even at home, the shinier and more inspiring the vision, the more vigor and commitment your players will bring. And the more that you can make your collective vision reflect elements of each team member's personal vision, the more passion they will bring to the project. They'll want to join you in making it succeed because it satisfies *them* too.

Tips for Making Your Vision Statements Glow

By now, I hope you see what a vision statement can do for you, and how richly you'll be rewarded for putting time and care into creating one. You started your visioning when you wrote your description of a perfect day and considered the elements that set it AGLOW. As we get ready to fold that work into your larger vision statement, I'll offer a few last guidelines.

- **Details matter:** A good vision statement draws you in and pumps you up with the enthusiasm you need to make it a reality. It doesn't need to be a piece of literary art, but it should include as many specifics as you can muster so that you can easily picture yourself doing the things you describe in an atmosphere that inspires you and brings you joy.

- **Positive language will give you more energy:** As I've said before, you are looking to feel empowered and excited, so pay close attention to how your chosen words make you feel. Try this experiment: state, in positive terms, how you are surrounded by people who get along with one another. The scene is serene and you are at ease. You are enjoying uncomplicated, effortless relationships with everyone in your life. It's an encouraging vision, right?

But how inspiring is this? "I am surrounded by troublemaking jerks, but they don't bother me much anymore. They aren't picking fights and making me quite as insane as usual. And, I can win the fights they do start." Do you find yourself holding your breath as you see these button-pushing words? See how much more encouraging the first version is than one that dwells on ridding yourself of negativity?

The words you use can have a profound impact on your emotions. This is the place to make them shiny and bright.

- **Give yourself time:** How far in the future should your vision be? That really depends on the distance between where you are and where you want to be. It could be a wide gap if you have a huge vision such as joining NASA and walking on the moon. You might want to pick a longer time line, too, if you're overcoming a setback, say recovering from a major surgery, and you've got some work to do just to prepare for your journey. Choose a time that seems reasonable for the size of your vision. Generally speaking, six months is a good lower boundary and five years is a reasonable upper limit.

You want to achieve this vision, of course, so you want the time frame to reflect steady, relentless progress toward your goal, but you don't want it to be so aggressive that you couldn't possibly meet the time frame and still have any joy in the journey. So give yourself some positive pressure, but don't go overboard and create one more source of unnecessary stress.

- **One page is a good goal:** My students often tell me that they've posted their mission and vision statements in a place where they can read them daily to stay focused and motivated. It's ideal if they are detailed and nuanced, but succinct enough so you can refer to them often for quick inspiration.

There's No One Right Answer

We all bring our own unique perspective to everything we do. We see things through our own lens, filtered through our own experiences. One view isn't right and another isn't wrong. The way we picture something is just a reflection of our perspective and worldview. Let me show you what I mean. Look at how the smallest shifts change your perception of the Koffka Ring[3] below. The gray ring is exactly the same in each of the three images even though it looks quite different as the background shifts and changes.

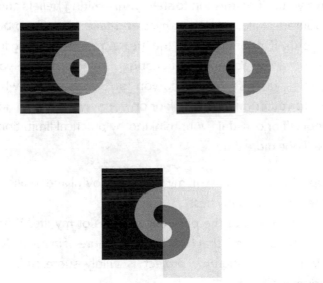

Is one perception right and another wrong? Not at all. The way you see something has everything to do with the way you look at it. The "right" vision is the one that's right for *you*.

EXERCISE

Your Personal Vision Statement: Weaving the Threads

Set aside some time when you will be free of phones, e-mail, and interruptions so you can quietly reflect. Read through the whole exercise and then review everything you wrote down as you worked through this chapter. It is time to weave all the threads of your vision into a tapestry that excites and inspires you.

You are defining your destination: Where are you headed on your map? Be very specific. What do you need for each day to be joyful as you move toward your destination? What does your life look like when you are using your special gifts in the way only you can?

Give yourself permission to shed your limiting beliefs and envision your ideal life. Close your eyes and take a few deep breaths. Place yourself at some point in the future. Your life is going just the way you want it. You wouldn't change a thing. What do you see, hear, smell, taste, feel? How do you look? Write down whatever comes to you in your notebook or on your computer. Do *not* censor yourself or constrain your thinking by practical limitations. Ask yourself one more time:

- What do I need to have in my life to feel joyful and fulfilled?
- When do I feel at my best?
- What are some of the peak experiences of my life? What was special about them that I want to have more of in my daily life?
- If I/my organization/my project is wildly successful, what is happening?
- If I didn't have to make money to live, how would I spend my time?
- Whose life do I envy? What do they have that I want in my life?
- Who are the people in my life who support my vision? How are they helping me? How am I interacting with them?

As you answer these questions, keep in mind that there is a difference between lasting joy and fleeting pleasure. Many people begin
this exercise with a fantasy of chilling on the beach with a frozen
umbrella drink, but soon come to the conclusion that doing that for
a lifetime would be rather meaningless. Pleasure is great, and you
should most certainly include a good dose of that in your vision.
But to be fully gratified and successful achieving your mission, you
will want to focus a fair bit of energy thinking about how you are
employing your special gifts to serve a conscious, worthy purpose.

Reflect on your responses to these questions and everything
else you've recorded. Write your personal vision statement incorporating all the elements that mean the most to you. Whatever you
have written, this is the kind of exercise you may want to allow to
marinate over a few days. Allow your vision to be present in your
thoughts when you are going for a walk, taking a shower, shaving,
or doing any repetitive, relaxing activity. You may want to keep
your notebook close at hand so you can take down any inspiring
thoughts that pop up when you're in a peaceful state and not forcing yourself to think about your vision. Inspiration can come at any
time, so be alert to thoughts, feelings, and signals. When an image
quickens your heartbeat and nudges the corners of your mouth
into a smile, pay attention to what's causing that excitement. It may
well be something that belongs in your vision.

Mini-Visions

I do a visioning exercise every day during my early-morning swim.
After my workout, I get into the pool for my cool-down and meditation. Using the rhythm of my breath and strokes to get into a relaxed,
focused state, I set an intention for each day. I think about what I want
to accomplish and how I want to feel. Then I concentrate on that
intention and what I need to do to make it happen. These are what I
call my "mini-visions."

I've got an overall vision statement for my life and business that is filled with details of what that all looks like as well as a vision for my typical day. (I started to type average, but of course, my vision is *aglow*, so my envisioned days are anything but average.) Now, in order to fulfill my big mission and vision, I have many small and medium-sized projects that need to be done. Each of these can have its own vision statement. At some point in the future, you may want to consider doing the same. For now, writing a vision statement for your overall mission is a great place to start.

Themes May Be Clear but the Specifics Are Elusive

Creating a vision statement can be a very abstract exercise for people who would naturally prefer to do, do, do and skip the dreaming phase. So how can a task-focused doer cross the vision statement off the to-do list? Start with what you know.

Lee Ann lost her cherished mother to cancer a few years ago. It was a wrenching heartache. When her beloved aunt was struck with the same fatal disease a short time later, Lee Ann couldn't justify staying in her successful management job, particularly since the last few years at work had become increasingly unfulfilling. She retired from her position and devoted herself to providing care, comfort, and companionship to her aunt during her illness. When her aunt passed away, Lee Ann was ready to resume her career, but didn't know what she wanted to do. It needed to be more meaningful, that much was clear. And she wanted to help people coping with cancer. That kernel of an idea, along with her firm commitment and intention, didn't add up to a full-blown vision, but it wasn't a bad place to start.

As we sat across the table from each other in her first coaching session, I asked her what brought her joy and what renewed her energy as she cared for her dying aunt. I also asked her what talents she drew on that gave her a sense of mission. Having no children of her own, she loved doing craft projects with her nieces. One of her favorite things was making killer Halloween costumes for the girls every year and she'd recently taken up painting to renew her spirit. She also said she is very organized and has a real talent for figuring out a series of steps needed to achieve her goals. She had drawn on these skills throughout her highly successful management career.

Neither of us knew where this combination of talents and passions would take her, but now she knew where to start looking. You will see as her story unfolds later in this book that her ability to articulate even a bit of what she wanted to do, and whom she wanted to help, would enable her to enlist the help of others to find a precise vision that fit.

So, if you're stymied, start with what you've got and write down whatever you can. Is there a specific group you want to serve? What activities bring you joy and satisfaction? What refills your spiritual cup? Go back to your talents and interests. What are you good at? What do you have to work with? Jot it all down. Don't push too hard. Enjoy some time just imagining yourself in an environment that juices you up. Get as specific as you can without straining. Then you may want to consider talking to some like-minded souls or other people you admire and start sharing the elements of your vision that you *can* describe.

Solicit the ideas, guidance, and suggestions of other people who may be able to help you round out your vision. There is no dishonor in asking for help. Keep on thinking, feeling, and talking, and be patient if it takes a while. Spend some time in quiet introspection. Give it regular thought and keep revisiting it until the pieces of your vision crystallize. Write them down as they come to you. This process should feel joyful as it unfolds. It's okay if it takes time, as long as you commit to sticking with it until a compelling vision comes into focus.

Now You'll Know You're on Track

Put the key elements of your vision into your custom closet, where you can look at them often and continue moving forward in your own special style—whether you're schussing down the slopes with exhilarating speed or striding over for a view of that waterfall you hear roaring in the distance. It's not unusual for people who have taken the Business of Life course to tell me that they're still pulling out their closets years after their class for inspiration and confirmation that they're still on the right track.

With a clear vision firmly in your mind's eye, you are ready to move to the next steps in the planning cycle: naming what you need to have in place to succeed and sizing up your ability to secure all you need to bring your vision to life.

Toolbox

Focus

We create our own reality, and what we think about, we bring about. This is not as metaphysical as you might think. You experience what you think about, so why not choose your thoughts deliberately? Cultivate the discipline to focus your thoughts on those experiences you want more of in your life and less on those you don't. Focus will also bring clarity and guide you to spend your precious resources getting the results you want.

Step ❸

Name Your Critical Success Factors

"Success is where preparation and opportunity meet."[1]
—Bobby Unser, Three-Time Indianapolis 500 Winner

You have created an ambitious, glowing vision, but perhaps it seems far off and out of reach. So now what? How do you go from dreaming to doing? The key is to examine the elements that set your vision aglow and to list everything you need to bring it to life. By writing it all down, you are taking a tangible step toward making real progress. This is a very brief but essential step. By accomplishing this simple task, you build positive forward momentum that moves you in the right direction before the glow dims and you go back to doing things the way you've always done them.

What You Need to Succeed

You already know where you're headed. If you were sketching out a map, your destination would be the vision you've so carefully created. It is time to get specific about what you need so you can figure out how you will make it happen. So, first things first: you will make a list. This step seems so obvious that many people skip right over it. But pausing for a moment to make sure you've documented what you need improves the odds that you will put everything in place to get where you're going.

You can't make a suit without taking careful measurements, creating a pattern, and procuring fabric, notions, and a sewing machine.

Your list of success factors will also help you assess the distance between where you are and where you're headed. In turn, that will help you see how far you have to travel and how long it might take to arrive.

Let's look at Raymond, the would-be concert pianist we met in earlier chapters. What would he need to fulfill that vision? With his ambition to be a musician of worldwide renown, here's a decent list of what he might need:

- Access to a piano
- A concert-level piano teacher
- Space to practice
- Aptitude for the piano
- Money to pay for the piano, space, and lessons
- Membership with an ensemble to practice with other musicians
- Knowledge of music theory

When Your Vision Seems Impossible to Achieve

Diane is a primary care physician at a highly traditional academic medical center. She came for some coaching as she considered the options for advancing her career while reserving ample time to spend with her two young daughters. As always, we began her planning with her creating an inventory of her strengths, interests, and values, and then she wrote her mission and vision statements. Thinking about how she could fulfill her vision overwhelmed her because she didn't have any role models who had done what she hoped to pull off for herself. She simply couldn't picture how to make it happen. Her vision included her cooking with her kids several nights a week and enjoying family dinners that they'd created as a team. Her husband, a busy attorney who shared this desire, was willing to commit to being home for those meals and offered to take on cleanup duty. That part seemed doable.

But Diane wanted to establish herself as a national thought leader in medicine, which, following the traditional career path, would require her to set up a research group, secure grants, and publish scholarly articles in prestigious journals. The problem with that scenario is that it didn't fit well with her busy primary care practice, to which she was passionately committed, and her active home life. Securing research funding is highly competitive and requires long hours in order to excel. Her ambition to have a soaring career while being an involved parent seemed impossible when held up against the realities of her chosen field.

I reminded Diane that until she fully explored all of her options, it was too early to dismiss her ideal as impractical and settle for something less. She was game to move forward, if not terribly optimistic. So I asked her to continue suspending disbelief for a while longer and just list what she would need to have in place for her to achieve this seemingly unworkable balance. She thought it might be more feasible to pull off this feat if she were able to do some of her work at home, so she came up with this list:

- A home office setup, with computer
- A morning clinical schedule that allowed her to be home after school hours
- Deep expertise in an issue of importance to her medical peers
- A platform to communicate her ideas
- The support of her division chief
- Salary for her nonclinical hours

Just committing her list to paper made it seem less overwhelming. While she still couldn't see how she would make this happen, she could begin to imagine how she might set some goals to further refine her vision. We'll meet up with Diane in the next step.

When You Don't Know Where to Start

If your vision is multifaceted, you may want to break it down into separate sections and make an inventory of success factors for each one. Organize them in whatever way works for you. I find it helpful to use different color markers to highlight the various parts of my vision, such as relationships, work, community, and mind/body/spirit pursuits. However you choose to approach this, make sure to include the joy notes that will make working toward your vision a pleasant journey.

Because my own vision encompasses many disparate yet harmonious activities, I have broken it down into projects and made a list of success factors for each one. For example, writing this book is one aspect of fulfilling both my personal and professional visions. I needed some obvious things:

- A computer
- Time, time, and more time to review and organize mountains of materials
- Welcoming work space
  - Attractive office with soothing colors
  - Clean, orderly desk
  - Inspiring photos
  - Pots of tea
  - Music
- Scheduled breaks for exercise and human contact
- Interviews with clients and program participants

This was also an opportunity to get some good "twofers"—activities that serve you in more than one way. Reviewing my vision statement was a great way to see the potential. When I rethought my writing schedule so that I could help my son prepare for his bar mitzvah, I had planned to get back on track by "going underground" to spend some concentrated time writing free from the competing demands of family, consulting projects, and coaching clients. A review of my vision statement reminded me that spending time in nature is critical to nourishing my spirit. Connecting with cherished friends is also central to my well-being, and is a particular challenge given the solitary nature of writing. So, I added to my list of critical success factors:

- Getting "off the grid" for five days
- Time in nature
- Good company for breaks

Just to show you where this is all leading, I'll jump ahead a couple of steps and demonstrate how this list of success factors led me to a strategy that fulfilled my whole list. I knew from past experience that trying to write for sustained periods from my office was a setup that would lead to distractions and frustration. Blocking off a few hours a day is usually doable, but the time required to get back on schedule meant that wasn't feasible. So, I decided to rent a cottage on Cape Cod for a few days and invite my sister to join me. The cape is very quiet and beautiful in the autumn and I was able to find a perfect space at off-season rates.

It was a magical time. I had the concentrated periods of quiet time I needed to reimmerse myself in this massive project and I had scheduled breaks for exercise and time in nature when we walked the beaches in the cool breeze. We were delighted by the rare opportunity to spend so much time together and we had the special treat of watching seals playing in the surf. The invigorating walks renewed me for a few more hours of writing. Then we capped off the day with dinner out. We made a point of testing the cosmopolitans in each restaurant we tried, so we accomplished some important research as well. Most important, I made up for lost writing time and returned home with renewed focus, successfully reconnected with this intense project.

Hopefully, it is now clear how listing your success factors will form a basis for creating strategies that are likely to help you achieve your goals. And, as important, to enjoy the process as much as is possible. So remember to add some spice and make your main course as delicious as it can be. Consider these factors as the ingredient list for your recipe for success.

EXERCISE

Make Your List

Pull out your vision statement and take a look all the individual aspects that comprise your ideal future. Grab your notebook and simply make a list of those things that need to be in place for you to fully occupy the picture you've drawn for yourself. Be as thorough as possible. In the next step, you will take an inventory of those factors that you have in place and those that you will have to acquire. The more detail you can develop here, the better your chances of getting them in place.

Step ❹

Find Your Sweet SWOT

"When I…use my strength in the service of my vision, it becomes less and less important whether I am afraid."[1]

—Audre Lorde

With your list of critical success factors in hand, it is natural to ask with some trepidation: Do I have what it takes to get there? A strategic plan doesn't leave you wondering. It gives you a clear, calm, and brilliantly easy way to find out. It's called a SWOT analysis. I don't have much use for business jargon, but I make an exception for SWOT, an acronym for strengths, weaknesses, opportunities, and threats. You can use your SWOT to size up what you have to work with—or work around—as you move into action on your project. With a clear picture of your assets and liabilities, you will be in a great position to figure out where to invest your efforts and resources so they will return the greatest dividends.

Size Up Your Position

Now comes a little reconnaissance. Is your vehicle the right one for the trip you want to take? Are there obstacles to steer around or particular routes that will send you flying toward where you want to go? A SWOT analysis will tell you, so you can plot out your next moves in a way that's custom designed to boost your chances for success.

The great thing about SWOT is its simplicity. It gives you a wealth of information by having you focus on just four key areas:

- Your strengths—the skills, talents, and resources you'll use to fulfill your vision.
- Your weaknesses—factors that could impede your progress. A weakness could be a skill or resource you need but don't have. It might also be a behavioral pattern that holds you back or a tendency to undermine yourself by doing things like thinking too small.
- Your opportunities—situations that could give you a chance to leverage your skills and talents.
- Your threats—outside factors that could get in your way.

You'll start by looking internally, at your own strengths and weaknesses. Next, you will scan your environment for potential opportunities and threats, the external factors that are out of your control but may have an impact on your success. Once you've recorded what you find, you'll be able to test how well your mission fits with your talents and circumstances, and evaluate the potential for challenges ahead. Armed with this information, you can set goals that will make the most of your assets and opportunities, fill in gaps, and mitigate potential threats.

Putting everything on a grid like the one below makes it easy to assess advantages and risks, and provides you with a checklist you can use when you set goals and create strategies to achieve them. Once again, by documenting key information, you reduce both the odds that you will forget something important and the anxiety that goes along with worrying that you'll drop a detail.

Internal factors	External factors
Strengths	Opportunities
Weaknesses	Threats

Will your trip toward your vision be easy or difficult? Your SWOT will reveal that at a glance so you can put yourself on track for success.

SWOT in a Nutshell

To see a SWOT in action, let's look at how Raymond's circumstances line up with his mission, vision, and critical success factors. Here's his list once again:

- Access to a piano
- A concert-level piano teacher
- Space to practice
- Aptitude for the piano
- Money to pay for the piano, space, and lessons
- Membership with an ensemble to practice with other musicians
- Knowledge of music theory

Strengths:	Opportunities:
• I live right down the street from the conservatory	• The conservatory has world-class instruments, practice space, and faculty
• My musical talent qualifies me for admission and a scholarship	• It has an ensemble orchestra for regular group practice and the camaraderie I need to enjoy the process

Weaknesses:	Threats:
• I lack the manual dexterity to play intricate pieces	• Federal funding for the arts may be cut, threatening my scholarship

Especially after working through his critical success factors, Raymond knew a lot about himself and the environment surrounding his vision. That intelligence is pulled together here.

When he looked at his SWOT, Raymond was reassured that he had the skills to be a great musician, and the fine conservatory recognized and rewarded his talent. But the SWOT forced him to consider a weakness he hadn't focused on much in the past; he didn't have the skill to play the piano at the level that would allow him to give full expression to his musical genius. As his fictional luck would have it, he learned he had arthritis and his fingers just couldn't fly over the keyboard at the speed needed to play Chopin concertos in allegro. Now what? Is his music career over? He felt surprisingly calm when he received the diagnosis.

This analysis drove Raymond to look at his options. He could try treating his condition and seek occupational therapy to shore up this weakness. Or he could go back and review his other strengths, and examine his mission and vision for alternatives. No wonder he was unruffled by his diagnosis. His mission "To beautify the world with musical harmonies that soothe the soul and ignite the spirit" did not require him to play the piano to fulfill it. Furthermore, when he looked at his vision statement, he was reminded that it is working with other musicians to create exquisite harmonies that really excites him. Finally, when he looked at his skills inventory, he recalled his unique ability to interpret great works and to imagine how to blend the many orchestral instruments to create arrangements that thrilled his audiences and fellow musicians. As he mused on his situation, he realized he'd been swept along by his father's expectation that his gifted son would have the piano career that had eluded him. That didn't fit with the authenticity that should define his own vision of his future. Here's what he realized when he revisited his vision statement to make sure it reflected his own definition of success:

I see myself surrounded by musicians and creating beautiful music with pianos, but, son of a gun, I don't need to be sitting at the piano to do that. As a conductor, I could blend magnificent harmonies and even a ham-fisted guy like me can wave a baton. My rhythm and timing are impeccable. What else do I need to succeed as a conductor and how do my strengths play into that? How would this shifted role play to my strengths? In addition to my great ear, it turns out I have a real knack for imagining how dozens of instruments can be layered on top of one another to create the most exquisitely nuanced version of a concerto the world has ever seen. Voilà! *That* is my true personal genius at work. My work will bring classical pieces alive and make fine music more accessible to the masses. The classical music industry, once in decline, has a shiny future, thanks to me. And to think, I once only wanted to play the piano.

Raymond's SWOT provided him with a reality check and an opportunity to make sure his ambitions really matched his passions and abilities. It offered him a chance for an early course correction that saved him from wasting precious time and effort pursuing an avenue that would never fulfill his vision of playing on the world music stage. In other words, he could choose a path that is likely to make the most of his strengths and give him some success to build on. He could also take advantage of the opportunities the conservatory offered and make contingency plans for alternative funding sources should his scholarship money dry up.

Notice that, as you move through the strategic planning process, you get steadily more concrete, attaching more detail and more analysis that's aimed at increasing the odds that the journey toward your vision will be full of wins and pleasure. The process is all about success.

EXERCISE

Swift SWOT

If you're a person who likes to skip the manual and get straight to assembling the furniture, feel free to do a preliminary SWOT of your project now, following the instructions in the exercise below. You can refine your SWOT as you move through the rest of this section. Draw a SWOT grid like the one above in your notebook or download a copy from joyofstrategy.com.

1. Take a look at your vision statement and your critical success factors. What strengths can you draw on that will position you for success? List them in the Strengths space.
2. What do you need to be successful that you don't have? List those missing ingredients in the Weaknesses box. Are you

doing anything (or not doing something) that undermines your objective? Add that as well.

3. What's happening around you that could present a great opportunity? Mark that down.

4. Do you perceive hazards in the environment that have the potential to blow you off course? Make a note of those issues in the Threats space.

SWOT Step by Step

The SWOT analysis is the point in the strategic planning process where we finish looking at who we are and prepare to think about what we *do*. And this completed self-assessment is the basis for all the action steps that come next. So now let's move through it element by element.

Strengths: Using Your Greatest Talents

In peak form, Michael Jordan flew down the basketball court, a perfect match of talent and passion, with results that put him in the record books. All that innate athletic ability, honed by focus, ambition, and hours of practice, landed him in the basketball pantheon. Did he have the strengths to be a basketball great? It seems absurd to ask. His remarkable skills and talents propelled him toward his mission and made him a star.

Now think back to Michael Jordan, baseball rookie. Same man, same talents. But notably, he was a man whose talents and skills were not the same tight match with his new sport. During that forgettable byway of his career, Jordan struggled for one lusterless season in the minors. And then he returned to the Chicago Bulls, a champion once more. As that humbling life experiment proved, he had enough raw athletic prowess to get through the door of another sport, but not enough to excel there. On the diamond, he was a jewel forced into the wrong setting. His talent was still beautiful, but it just didn't fit.

Your talents can wax the slide for you, and they can send you on the ride of your life—as long as they're a good match for your mission. When the fit is right, they're strengths. When it's not, you might just feel like Michael Jordan in a batting helmet.

The strengths part of a SWOT is a place where you can see how much your talents are stacking the deck in favor of success with the direction you've chosen. The more specific skills you have that support your vision, the more your journey will be a smooth, swift arc toward your target. No forced effort, just a natural expression of who you are and what you do best.

The "Stuff" of Strengths

Obviously, success takes more than talent. You'll also need other things, like time, materials, money, and staff. The resources you have in hand are *also* strengths, and of course you'll need to take them into account. Your talents and skills, though, are what turn stuff into results.

The skills and resources you need for your vision are spelled out right there on your list of Critical Success Factors, so there's no need for guesswork. You can get a good picture of your strengths by going down the list item by item and answering the question: Do I have it? Every "Yes" is a specific strength related to reaching your vision.

Peggy and Gail were encouraged and energized when they saw how many strengths they had for opening Our Space, their arts center for kids with cancer. As they started their SWOT, they could see a kind of critical mass building. Every time they confirmed that they had one of their critical success factors, it felt like an affirmation. And it was. Their "yeses" are listed in the "Do we have it?" column:

Skill/Resource We Need	Do We Have It?
Ability to attract critical mass of parents and kids interested in our services	1. We have an inspiring mission and vision. 2. We're strong advocates with a good message. 3. Our research revealed a receptive group of kids and families facing cancer.

(Cont.)

Skill/Resource We Need	Do We Have It?
Service providers: teachers, therapists, yoga instructors, artists	Yes: we are teachers ourselves and our network of colleagues is full of people willing to volunteer their services
Art supplies	We own a lot of supplies and we know several others who are willing to donate even more to help sick kids

Looking at the list of strengths you bring to your project can give you a great sense of confidence. It can also give you information that could nudge you in a new direction. Or, like Michael Jordan on his baseball detour, you might discover that your proposed mission, wonderful as it is, isn't the best match for your unique talents. Pay attention if you don't have a solid "I'm on the right track" feeling when you finish listing your strengths. Those strengths are the fuel for your journey.

EXERCISE

Record It

Go through your Critical Success Factors and for each one, as Peggy and Gail did, answer yes or no to the question, "Do I have it?" The details you put under each "yes" answer are strengths. Put them in the Strengths section of your SWOT grid.

Weaknesses: Skills or Resources You Lack

As you went through the inventory above, looking at the skills and resources you need for your project and answering the question "Do I have it?" Your eye may have been drawn to the spots where the answer was no. The "nos" are weaknesses.

A weakness can be a skill or resource you need for your project that you don't have. It might also be an inner quality, such as fear or a bad habit, that's holding you back. Building a house but don't have lumber? That's a weakness. Lack of carpentry skills would be too, as would a fear of hammers.

The very word weakness makes many people uncomfortable, but keep in mind that a SWOT doesn't judge, it simply tells you what you need so you can decide how you'd like to get it. Do you feel bad about yourself if you don't happen to have fresh pineapple in your fridge, but need it for a recipe? Probably not—you just put pineapple on your shopping list. And that's how it works with weaknesses. You spot them and you address them.

One assumption I'd like you to take off the table is that you have to be a one-person show who can—or should—do everything yourself. Weaknesses are often areas that don't tap your personal genius, and that's invaluable information for you to have. Remember that a strategic plan is all about finding ways to use your resources wisely. You'll get the best results if you put your time, energy, and focus into areas that make the most of your talents. The rest you can hand off to someone who can do the job better.

As a person who really likes to be able to say, "I can handle that," I know that it can be tough to admit that you're not the perfect person for every job. But I can tell you that there is grace in letting go of the notion that you have to do everything yourself. It's a relief. Once you know what has to get done, and acknowledge what part of it lies outside your wealth of talents, you can find help. There's probably someone whose strengths are a perfect match for your weakness.

I could do a decent job on my accounting if I really wanted to file my taxes on my own. It would certainly save me money. But I'd have to invest a lot of time because I'm not experienced enough to do it efficiently. Not to mention that I'm anything but passionate about adding up columns of numbers. Knowing this about myself, I can figure out what's in shorter supply: time or money, and then decide the best use of my resources. I'm not flawed because tax codes leave me cold, I'm just wired differently from those remarkable souls who love to curl up with the latest tax-rule changes. Fortunately, some of those tax mavens see their mission as helping poor schlubs like me stay on the good side of the IRS. My weakness is their strength, and a happy partnership is born.

Your Strategic To-Do List Is Taking Shape

I've described how energized Peggy and Gail were when they looked at their array of strengths for their arts drop-in center. That was a good thing, too, because they began to panic a bit when they got to weaknesses. But they were doing a strategic plan in the first place because they felt stuck when it came to making their vision come alive. This exercise showed them why that was and gave them clues to what to do about it. The "nos" in the "Do we have it?" column below reflect Peggy and Gail's weaknesses:

Skill/Resource We Need	Do We Have It?
Space to create and connect	No, and space is expensive
A step-by-step start-up plan	1. We have no idea where to start, or what to do to get our center out of our heads and into the real world
	2. We don't know how to plan
	3. We lack experience starting a business
Start-up cash	1. We don't have any extra money for this
	2. We don't have fundraising experience
	BUT
	1. Gail is a stand-up comic with the gift of gab; she'd be great at fundraising if she tried
	2. We also have artwork of our own that we could auction off or sell to raise cash
	3. We know a lot of people who will help us with fundraising
Publicity/marketing	We need help with a website, graphics, and printing

The pair, usually so full of energy and laughter, almost physically deflated as they confronted this litany of "nos." "Arggh," Gail moaned, head in her hands. "I knew this was just pie in the sky. Look at us. We're artists. This really brings it home—we don't know the first thing about starting a business."

That was one truth, I told her, but there was another: now that they were clear about what they lacked, they could find ways to get it. They had actually begun doing that automatically when they listed their obstacles with start-up cash. Even as they were writing down their weaknesses on that front, they could see that they had strengths and opportunities there, too. Not cash—not yet—but ideas for raising it. When you see yourself wrestling with a particular item on the weakness list, it's a strong sign that the issue is so important to the overall success of the project that it's really an undertaking of its own.

The real stoppers on your weaknesses list, the ones that knock the air out of you, often deserve deeper attention. Peggy and Gail finished the SWOT for Our Space, then went back to do a separate SWOT for the financing piece, so they could look more closely at the opportunities they sensed there. And those "buts" they had noted on their list of weaknesses, they realized, were strengths.

EXERCISE

Record It

Go back to your Critical Success Factors "Do I have it?" list and transfer the details you put under each "no" answer to the Weaknesses section of your SWOT grid. Note any "big" weaknesses that might benefit from a SWOT of their own.

Your Weakness Is Someone Else's Strength

As so often happens, serendipity was afoot as Peggy and Gail faced their weaknesses. Talking with them about their lack of planning skills, I found myself thinking about my client Lee Ann. She's the manager we met earlier who was looking for a way to return to work in a meaningful way after leaving her high-level job to care for her aunt as she succumbed to cancer. Lee Ann, a gifted project manager, was extraordinary in her ability to translate a vision to reality, but after she lost her aunt, she couldn't see the path that would let her express her new mission: to use her skills to help cancer patients in a meaningful way.

One answer, though, was right in front of us. Peggy and Gail's puzzle was missing a piece shaped exactly like Lee Ann, and her puzzle was missing a piece shaped just like them. I arranged to bring the three of them together. As if to confirm that the universe was at work in making the connection, when Lee Ann pulled into the parking lot for her first meeting with Peggy and Gail, she saw a car—that turned out to be Peggy's—with a bumper sticker that read "Grace Happens." It was the very bumper sticker she kept in the glove compartment of her own car as a tribute to her mother, Grace. Tingling, and covered in goose bumps, Lee Ann went in to meet with the visioneers of Our Space.

She was dazzled by the artists' energy, craft, and vision, and also by their appreciation as she walked them through the first steps of finding support for their center and breaking down a huge, daunting project into manageable steps. With her guidance and coaching, they learned the basics of project management and gained the confidence to take action in unfamiliar areas to support their vision.

They also gave Lee Ann an important and unexpected gift: a new perspective on her talents. Often, we assume that the skills that come so easily to us are easy for everyone. But in meeting Peggy and Gail, who were astonished by her ability to handle their business planning, Lee Ann was able to see her talents as the distinctive gift they really are. That gave her the clarity and confidence to envision her own next steps.

You become part of a much larger circle when you match your weaknesses with someone else's strengths. For that to happen, though, you have to take a look at what you lack and what you need. Then ask for help.

Are You Getting in Your Own Way?

There's a group of weaknesses that can be a little trickier to see than a simple accounting of what you need and don't have. These are the fears and limiting beliefs that keep you from using your talents fully. Behavior patterns that often find their roots in fear can be so familiar to you that you may not even notice them. What you might perceive instead is that while you have all the strengths and opportunities you need to glide toward your vision, something keeps pulling you off track. That "something" is often fear.

Seven Fears That Can Block the Way

In my work as a senior executive, teacher, and coach, I've identified several patterns of self-defeating behavior people indulge at the expense of achieving their goals. Take a look at some of the most common fear-based behaviors below. Do you see yourself in one or more of these patterns or personality types? I ask this question with great compassion and empathy, as many of us struggle with one or more of these issues. Treat this exploration as another simple inventory. And if you recognize yourself, treat that knowledge as valuable information that will bring you closer to your vision.

1. People Pleasing

The inability to say no may well be the most common problem that diverts people from their own goals. People with the disease to please say yes a lot when they mean no because they fear disappointing someone. My client, Jim, was so worried about disappointing his parents that he went to law school even though he dreaded the very thought. Without some new strategies, he could easily have spent a lifetime in a career he hated, wondering why he felt so empty—and why he still hadn't won the approval of those for whom he'd sacrificed so much.

This problem is particularly prevalent among people in the healing professions. I've worked with countless doctors and nurses whose identity is so connected to helping others that they often put their own needs behind everyone else's. That would be okay if it didn't lead to burnout and resentment, which it frequently does.

2. Perfectionism

My client Miranda was a top executive, superb at execution, completing tasks, even identifying vision. But she was also extremely hard on herself and others, ferocious when she or anyone under her fell short of her unreachable expectations. She found money and prestige but very little satisfaction until she took some rare time for introspection and realized she'd spent her life driven by the need to win her parents' approval. She believed that they wouldn't love her unless she was perfect, and "perfect" was always just out of reach.

3. Inertia

Danielle, the unhappy fashionista we met earlier, managed to spend two decades in a career she hated. How could that happen? Fear of leaving her familiar gilded cage, with its high salary, honors, perks, and benefits, had prevented her from taking a hard look at the truth that she confronted every day even though she tried not to think about it: she was miserable. And because she'd been afraid to admit it, she had condemned herself to keep going mindlessly until a string of difficult days added up to an unhappy twenty years.

4. Ego Identification and Control Issues

Another client, Angie, quit her job as a bank vice president when her first child was born so she could spend time nurturing her beautiful baby and enjoying her growing family. Soon enough, though, she was channeling every bit of her business drive into her kids' schools and organizations, which she turned into a full-time job. All because she couldn't turn off the chatty ego voice inside that wanted her to look good, keep up appearances, impress. She was afraid of giving herself over to the "unglamorous" job of simply being Mommy and so, ironically, had little time left for her children. She was too busy volunteering.

5. Listening to Naysayers

Remember Brenda, the woman we met in step 1, the "Mission" chapter, who was told by a teacher way back in middle school that she was no good in math? It was an assessment she never challenged. She simply crossed off the list any path that required her to use numbers. But after years of denial and misguided career choices, she finally faced the fact that she couldn't have the career in management she'd always wanted without a college degree—and getting a degree required, *gasp,* taking some math courses.

6. Succumbing to the Yeah-But Habit

For Stella, a student in my Business of Life course, every big dream seemed to come with a whole army of reasons why it was impossible to pull off. The "yeah-buts" popped up all over, and the funny thing is, with her confirmed yeah-but habit, they seemed to be a sign of realism rather than pessimism or a block. But beneath it all was fear—fear of failure, embarrassment, wasted effort. Or fear that what she wanted most in life just "wasn't meant to be."

7. Procrastination

So much to do, so little time for what's important. That's the dilemma of the chronic procrastinator. Easily distracted by the Crackberry, e-mail, web surfing, other people's conversations—and any number of other wheel-spinning diversions—people like my client Jerry are, paradoxically, busy, busy, busy. They're the ones who careen from one task to another all day, yet go home without accomplishing a single thing of value to them. One of the characteristics of a workaholic is procrastination. Eastern philosophers call this paradox active laziness, a way many people avoid looking deep inside to see what's really important. Procrastination keeps them from focusing on tasks that could have an impact and use their real talents. Most of us procrastinate from time to time without serious repercussions. But the fear of many habitual procrastinators is that their vision is too big, too hard, or too impossible, and they just can't risk failing. Or even starting.

Toolbox

Mirror

Pause a moment for some honest self-reflection. Look in the mirror or quietly close your eyes and ask yourself if you have any fear-based habits that are standing in the way of fulfilling your dreams.

For our purposes, how any of us wound up with these patterns isn't important. That's in the past, and we are here, right now, in the present. The goal is to move from where you are to where you want to be, and recognizing these patterns is the first step toward breaking free of them. If you can keep your focus there, putting aside judgment or labeling, you liberate the energy these patterns can trap and channel it in a more productive direction.

If you notice one of these patterns is at work in your life, one helpful thing to do is to consider what it's costing you. Often, I frame the situation this way for a client: What's more important to you? That Patsy, whom you'll never see again, will like you better because you made brownies for the school bake sale or that you write your novel? Are you pouring your energies into something that will never satisfy you, just to tiptoe around a fear?

Use the weaknesses section of your SWOT to identify what might be going on in your inner world that could be hindering your progress. You can unearth causes later and figure out how to address any problems. For now, knowledge is the first step to change and to reclaiming your power. Put a checkmark next to any of the patterns that resonate with you, and we'll return to them. And if one of these patterns is causing you deep distress, keep in mind that one highly effective strategy might be to work on it with a therapist, even as you continue building your strategic plan.

EXERCISE

Record It

Do you find that you act in ways that are not working for you? Mark it on your weaknesses list. Just a brief note, such as "I procrastinate" or "people pleasing," will suffice.

Opportunities and Threats

If our visions existed in a vacuum, we could boil down SWOT to SW (though it might be a little tough to say). But the cherished projects we conjure up in our minds are meant to be carried into the world. And out there, many factors are beyond our control. A SWOT takes them into account with an external analysis that helps you identify the factors that could smooth your way and even put some wind in your sails, so you can take advantage of them. Or anticipate those things that could impede you, so you can steer around them or push them aside.

For a company that makes sports caps and equipment, the Olympics might be an incredible opportunity to offer new products or snag an endorsement contract. And for a wedding planner in an Olympic host city, the weeks surrounding the games might be a threat that makes it hard to book venues and get attention. Or perhaps they'd be a great chance to offer sports-themed ceremonies. These imaginary businesses have no control over the timing of the Olympics or the ripples it sends into the environment. But they can anticipate and adjust their planning. Scanning the environment and becoming aware of the outside forces that can affect them, they gain an advantage that will let them surf the big waves or get out of the water before the typhoon hits.

As Jimmy Dean once said, "I can't change the direction of the wind, but I can adjust my sails to always reach my destination."[2] So let's do that. We'll look at opportunities and threats together, because the difference between an opportunity and a threat often depends on your point of view.

Opportunities

When a vision takes hold in your mind, much of the excitement surrounding it comes from seeing a need in the world for what you do best. You feel the pull of your calling. When you keep your focus there, on the match between your talents and the world's needs, you'll naturally begin to see situations with your name written on them, problems with solutions *you* can provide.

Remember the definition: an opportunity is a situation that gives you a chance to leverage your skills and talents. That's what you'll be looking for all around you.

Stella's dream was to open a religious bookstore that would create community and spread the wisdom and comfort she found in her beliefs. With her "yeah-but" tendencies, she felt stymied. After all, she said, she needed to keep her day job, with its steady paycheck and health benefits, so fulfilling her dream was out of the question.

I asked her if she'd considered running the store part time herself and hiring someone to mind the store while she was at work. "Yeah," she replied, "but I can't afford the rent and the salary until the store starts turning a profit, and I really want to keep my prices low so anyone can have access to the message in these books."

I counseled Stella to keep her eyes open and hold her vision of the bookstore so firmly in her mind that she would be open to interpret anything she saw in her daily travels as an opportunity to make her dream come alive. She kept pulling her mind toward her vision, and that very weekend, when she went to church, she saw her first big opportunity, one that had been right under her nose for years. Her church was located on a busy corner in the downtown section of a city with lots of foot traffic. The front door to the sanctuary was on one street, and the church building had an empty storefront on the perpendicular street. Stella recalled that the minister had long been concerned that the vacant display windows would invite vandalism.

After services, Stella approached the minister and asked him what he would think of her opening a bookstore in that empty space, with hours on weekends and a few selected evenings. He was delighted with the idea that the space could be used to further the church's mission and would make the space look occupied and less vulnerable to vandals. He offered her the opportunity to use the space rent-free, and she offered to donate a portion of her profits to the church.

She was overjoyed. The power of holding her vision firmly in her mind's eye had proven itself immediately. That old saying, "What you focus on, you find," is quite true. If you put your attention on something, it's possible that you draw the "pulling power of the universe." What's certain is that you draw on the power of your own vision by keeping alert to the possibilities to make it happen.

Coincidence—like meeting someone who knows a person you need a connection to, or suddenly being offered a gift that provides just what you were seeking—feels like serendipity. But I think it's often focus finding opportunity. There are plenty of opportunities staring us in the face if we're focused enough to see them.

EXERCISE

Seize Opportunities

Think about the factors in the world around you that could support your vision: helpful people, events you've noticed, anything that might potentially give your project a boost. List these opportunities on your SWOT grid. Then spend a week keeping your vision in front of you (read it every morning, or set a reminder on a calendar that prompts you to think about it). As the week unfolds, be open to interpreting anything you see as an opportunity to bring your vision to life. As ideas occur, keep adding to your list of opportunities.

Threats

The best-laid plans can be derailed by factors large and small. Life happens. The price of gas triples just as you're getting ready to open your Humvee franchise. A stock market bubble bursts. A Starbucks announces that it's opening across from your mom and pop coffee house. You have no control over outside events like this, but by being aware of your environment and the forces that threaten to derail your journey toward your vision, you can tailor your responses, tweak your plans, even find a catalyst for inspired new possibilities.

So if the idea of actively looking for "threats" sounds too, well, threatening, think of it this way: you're living out the old Boy Scout motto that smartly advises "Be prepared." Putting your head in the sand won't make the threats go away. But as we'll see, examining them closely, or standing them on their heads, just might.

Businesses commonly scan the horizon for what the competition is up to, how their current and potential clients might be changing, and what's going on with new laws, regulations, and technology. For your SWOT, look around the wider world that surrounds your project and see what could have a negative impact. Your threats could include someone who doesn't support your vision for whatever reason, like a spouse who would rather see you stay home and clean house than pursue a dream. Or it could be something less intimate: the credit crisis that makes cash hard to come by or the rainy season coming to drown out your lemonade stand.

If you have "yeah-but" inclinations that tend to make the environment look especially threatening, use this opportunity to list every possible element that could take the spark out of your project. That will enable you to deal with each one in a methodical, practical way instead of staying paralyzed. Threats, by definition, are factors that are out of your control, but you are very much in control of how you interpret and respond to them. The first step is to look for them and name them. Then you can make plans to deal with them.

As Peggy and Gail looked around for threats, their list was short—one big, overarching threat and another one that helped them think about how they might want to use one of the opportunities they'd pinpointed.

Peggy and Gail's threats:

- The economy is still slumping, so all those foundations and individuals who used to have a lot of money to give have less. There's a lot of competition when it comes to fundraising, and we're going to need money to establish ourselves.
- We will eventually need a permanent space, and real estate is very expensive. It may get even more expensive before we've gotten our fundraising skills up to speed.

"Hmm, this doesn't seem so terrible," Gail said. "It's more about knowing the possibilities than anything else. I don't like the word 'threats,' and these things we turned up are just potential problems. Besides, we already knew they were there. All we've done is written them down so we can figure out how to deal with them. It's less scary than I thought."

EXERCISE

Capture the Threats

List any outside factors that have the potential to throw your journey toward your vision off track. Are there people, events, or situations that could have a negative impact? Put them in the threats section of your SWOT.

Is That Hazard Really a Threat?

I'm a threat skeptic. When people suggest that a situation is dire, that some turn of events has blasted a hole in their boat and their vision is going down, I'm sympathetic, but I'm also inclined to ask: Really? Are you sure? In fact, are you sure you even need a boat to get where you're going?

I've seen many times that one person's threat is another's opportunity. Does every cloud have a silver lining? Well, maybe not. But if you've ever talked to someone ramping up a cleanup business after a natural disaster or watched people take a difficult experience (say, going through chemotherapy for cancer) and transform it into an inspiring vision ("let's create a center to help kids getting chemo"), you know the power of perspective.

Reframing

Look at your *conclusions* about the situation you've labeled a threat and ask: "Are you absolutely sure this is a threat?" You will need to learn the difference between assessing a fact (the economy is tanking) and your conclusions (we're doomed). Once you do that, the fact is just a fact and you can consider it objectively and reframe your reaction.

The trick to reframing is to question all of your limiting beliefs and to not simply believe the naysayers, as Brenda did with her math phobia. How do you do that? It's as simple as recasting yourself as an observer. With a little objectivity, you can resist jumping to "obvious" conclusions and can ask several questions that allow you to find more creative answers. With Brenda, we reframed her certainty that she was not good at math by asking if that was really true. Yes, her middle school teacher made that assertion, but what did the evidence show? In fact, her job responsibilities required her to create elaborate spreadsheets and to track complex statistics. She did it so naturally that she didn't even realize her facility with figures was actually a *strength*. Her only weakness in this regard was her misperception that she didn't possess this talent. Her new awareness eliminated that weakness for the most part. It was with some trepidation that she recorded math in the strengths quadrant of her SWOT.

I found myself using reframing to good effect after the stock market crashed in 2008 and the economy tanked. A lot of coaches I know panicked, certain that no one would be able to afford the luxury of hiring a coach. That sounded logical on the surface. But as I centered myself and looked around, I asked the questions I coach my clients to use: Does this situation, bad as it looks, create a new opportunity? Does it create a need my talents can fill?

That's when I began to notice the glut of talented financial services professionals who'd been laid off, all of them now competing for the same handful of jobs in their shrinking field. How could they stand out? How could they use the opportunity of a career transition to assess what they wanted to do in the next stage of their careers? Those are the kinds of questions I specialize in helping people answer, and in the context of this new environment, I found lots of opportunities— speaking about "personal branding" to professional groups, coaching people through job transitions. I had as much business as I could possibly handle, even as many others threw up their hands, positive that they were no match for an economic meltdown.

Reframing takes practice, but it's worth the effort.

Roadblock or Vantage Point?

A boulder in the road is a big piece of rock. That's a fact. But is it a threat? That depends. If you're driving fast and don't see it soon enough, yes. It's a big, potentially fatal threat. But if you're walking, the same boulder might give you a chance to climb up, survey the landscape, and figure out the easiest way to proceed. Perspective is everything. So take a close look at every threat on your SWOT. Hidden there, waiting for you to see it, might be an amazing opportunity.

EXERCISE

Test Your Assumptions

For every threat on your list, ask yourself these questions:

- What is the *fact* of the perceived threat?
- What is my assumption/conclusion about that threat?

- Is that assumption correct?
- How do I know?
- Can I be sure?
- Is there something I can do to change the fact?
- What is another way to interpret the implications of the fact?
- How else could I look at this?

Did you find new possibilities that flip your threat into the opportunities column? If so, note the changes on your grid. You'll have a chance to practice much more with reframing in step 7 when you assemble your toolkit.

When the SWOT Delivers News You Didn't Expect

Now that you've got all the pieces of your SWOT, you have an intimate feel for the terrain you'll be traveling. And at this point, it occasionally happens that people realize that they're in for such a rough trip they're on the wrong journey. That is, they've chosen the wrong mission. You can fool yourself with a fantasy, but it's hard to fool a SWOT.

Mission Misfit

I like to give my students the following scenario so they can see the value in a SWOT that lets them know when the strengths they need for a mission just aren't there. Say I've always wanted to win the Miss America Pageant, and I've put that goal at the center of my mission. Tall, lithe blondes have an advantage in the competition, and I'm five two and brunette, so a quick SWOT might reveal that I have no real strengths except for being Miss Congeniality, and I've got a boatload of weaknesses: height, age, gravity…I can't think of many opportunities, and the threats abound—thousands of tall, thin, young blondes, for example.

This SWOT would probably send me scurrying to reconsider what my mission ought to be. And that's not a bad thing. It means the SWOT served its function, alerting me that perhaps beauty contests are not the place where my talents and passions intersect with the needs of the world. (The world does *not* need to see me in the bathing suit competition, I assure you.) This kind of SWOT might well be painful, but it could save me a lot of useless effort and expense trying to become something I'm not.

The truth is, you probably won't get to the point of doing a SWOT analysis only to discover that your mission is so far off base. Certainly, in doing an assessment of my skills, talents, and passions, I wouldn't have found the stuff of beauty queens. And when I set to work on my vision statement, I wouldn't have gotten past the A in "AGLOW." There is nothing authentic about my chasing after a pageant title. It's not at all true to who I am and what I value most. Chances are, if you complete your SWOT and find you need to change direction, you are looking at a more modest redirection rather than a total reboot.

Alternative Approach

Annette came to me for coaching when she couldn't get traction on her mission to work with medical practices to provide a more holistic approach to patient care. She was particularly interested in advocating for progressive health policies and insurance coverage for nonmedical interventions such as in-home support for people who need help buying groceries and filling prescriptions. When we reviewed Annette's strengths, she had passion for this issue, having seen how the medical community fell far short of meeting her husband's needs when he was terminally ill. Insult was heaped upon injury when he lost his rich health benefits once he was no longer able to work—just when he needed them most.

She was driven to make sure others didn't suffer the same fate. Her intimate knowledge of the problem she was trying to solve was another strength, as was the faith she'd leaned on to get through her ordeal.

However, when I asked her how these strengths would bring value to a medical practice such that they would want to hire her for this worthy purpose, she was hard-pressed to give a compelling answer. What she was offering appealed to some providers in principle, but that wasn't much of an opportunity. And the growing pressure for doctors to cut medical costs was a real threat. The pieces just didn't fit.

Annette already knew this on some level and the SWOT just confirmed it. But before she had time to get discouraged, I asked her to expound more on the faith she kept mentioning and her conviction that this was a calling that came from a higher authority. She became so animated that I had to stop her and ask her to reconsider whether she wanted her nonprofit to work in partnership with doctors' offices or whether running a religious organization was more in harmony with her mission to advocate for patients. Without hesitation, she said this was a faith-based pursuit.

Immediately, she had much more clarity about how she could move forward gathering support for this reframed endeavor. Her SWOT redirected her by showing how her initial approach wasn't a great fit for her strengths and circumstances. When she factored in all the pieces of her SWOT, Annette was able to find a better way to address her mission. As a result, her next steps became obvious and she was able to move forward after years of being stuck.

Harmonizing with Your Strength and Passion

You're looking for a mission, a vision—a life—that will let you be a star, a great fit with your talents and values. So if you find yourself getting a troubling message from your SWOT analysis, take a deep breath and have another look at your strengths and passions. You deserve a mission that makes the most of them, and it's worth investing the time to find it. Like Raymond, you just might find that your mission calls for you to play even bigger than you'd originally envisioned. He had to question an assumption about how he would express his musical gifts, namely that his father would fulfill his own musical dreams vicariously through his son. Pursuing that path would have meant falling short of his true potential. The apparent misfortune of arthritic joints saved him from pursuing the wrong path.

EXERCISE

Sum Up the SWOT

Be sure you have captured all of your SWOT information on your grid, where you can pull it out and refer to it as needed. As you complete your self-assessment and move toward goal setting, finish filling out the left-hand side of your custom closet. Make sure you put any core strengths or talents you've found in this chapter on the appropriate shelf for easy reference as you move to the next step in the process.

Peggy and Gail's final SWOT analysis looked like this, and as we saw above, new opportunities began presenting themselves almost as soon as the two artists began looking for them. Weaknesses were answered by new strengths.

Strengths	Opportunities
• Inspiring mission and vision	• Vision fills an important void
• Strong, creative, passionate advocates	• Growing awareness that children with cancer have special needs that are unmet by medical field or other providers; that should help with fundraising
• Big network, comedy skills, and art collection to support fundraising effort	
• Excellent staff and supplies	

Weaknesses	Threats
• We are disorganized and don't know what steps to take to incorporate	• Struggling economy may impede fundraising
• No business planning experience	• Real estate is very expensive even in a depressed market, and prices may rebound before we get a handle on fundraising; that would mean even more trouble finding affordable space
• Need help with website, graphics, printing	

By just putting the potential threats to their endeavor on paper, Peggy and Gail began to see ways to address the problems and find alternate ways to deliver services much faster than they'd originally envisioned. We will catch up with Peggy and Gail later to see what they were able to accomplish.

Postscript: Keep SWOT in the Lineup

Now that you know the basics of performing a SWOT analysis, you'll find that it's a versatile tool for getting an overview of a problem or project and figuring out what needs attention. If your undertaking is complex, like starting a new business or changing careers, you might want to break it down and perform multiple SWOTs of individual elements.

Here's how: take out your vision statement and list of critical success factors. Underline the key elements and assess your strengths, weaknesses, opportunities, and threats for each one. Don't get too hung up on getting it "perfect." As you've seen, perfectionism can be a weakness when it comes to getting things done.

No need to get swamped in SWOTs. Just keep the tool in your back pocket and pull it out whenever you need the perspective it can bring. The process is dynamic, and focusing on the information you've collected here will lead you directly to setting smart, effective goals and priorities, the task of the next step in the process.

Step ⑤

Set Goals: Your Steps to Success

"Vision without action is a daydream. Action without vision is a nightmare."

—Japanese proverb

You have done a lot of important work, so take a moment to pause, reflect, and acknowledge what you've already accomplished. Don't worry that you're not "finished." As long as you're living and growing, you never will be. That's a good thing. You can go back to the foundational steps you have just completed and update them at any time as new information, experiences, circumstances, and feelings arise. This is a dynamic process that invites regular reviews and adjustments.

Up until now, your work has been to do some strategic soul-searching and analyze what you need to succeed in the business of your life. Your vision statement describes what success means to you and your critical success factors are a list of things you'll need to make it come to life. Your SWOT (strengths, weaknesses, opportunities, and threats) summed up your position and provided you with intelligence about what you have to work with and work around. So you now have a great foundation on which to build an action plan.

A vision is just a pretty picture until you actively breathe life into it. Your prioritized list of goals gives you a wonderfully effective way to think about how you'll want to spend your precious resources of time, energy, money, and attention that works in harmony with your core values, mission, and vision over time. The next step is to determine what you need to *do* to make real, steady progress toward living your envisioned ideal. That includes finding pleasure in each day while you work on getting "there." To do that, you will set some goals. Accomplishing them will give you an energy boost and keep you moving forward. Especially when some of those goals include spending more time with people you love or having a peanut butter and pickle sandwich every day if that's your thing.

Later in this chapter, we will look at how to make your goals as effective as possible. Taking the time in the goal-setting phase to ensure they are specific, measurable, and timely will make it possible to create successful strategies for accomplishing them and tracking your progress toward fulfilling your vision.

These early steps were just what Sandra needed to get motivated to work in a more holistic manner. Because of her left-brained, "let's get it done" tendencies, the conceptual work involved in creating a vision gave her focus and brought her pleasure as she contemplated a fulfilling future. For someone so task-oriented, it provided a well-rounded basis for setting goals and choosing carefully considered tasks likely to bring her great results as she crossed them off her list. Creating a vision did two other important things for her:

- She noticed that among the many aspects of her personal vision, she felt a particular urgency to launch Fertility Within Reach, her nonprofit organization that aims to empower infertile couples to advocate for themselves in order to build their families.

- She realized that, as a leader, she had been "pretty loose" about project management and, as a result, several initiatives languished. Involving her team in creating a collective vision for their department created a new sense of commitment to their work. Setting clear goals to make it happen was an important motivator and those goals were the basis for establishing the accountability needed to keep herself and her group on target. She no longer leaves it to chance.

Sandra's SWOT told her a lot about her considerable assets—strengths she needed to leverage and opportunities she could seize.

She also confronted a weakness she'd never really looked at as such until performing this analysis. Sandra, who is mindful in many ways and extraordinarily effective in completing projects, discovered that her way-too-long to-do list spread her attention too thin and threatened her ability to concentrate enough effort on her highest priorities. This was an important wake-up call and something she could readily address. Her vision statement snapped her right into focus and guided her next steps.

Move from Dreaming to Doing

Formulating goals is the step that creates the bridge between dreaming and doing. As you will see, the more specific you can be about what you will do to bring your vision to life, the more likely you are to do it. Your goals articulate *what* you want to accomplish. The strategies you will develop specify *how* you will accomplish it all. For now, your job is to get clear on what you want to do. Many people get so hung up on how they will get things done that they get stuck right here. If you're not clear on what you want, it will be hard to figure out how to get it. So, your task for this step is to stay focused on setting your goals. Once again, the key is to not cut off your options too soon by worrying about how you will achieve them. That is the work of the next step.

Bruce is the strategic planner whose vision included having a third child. He had a hard time committing his vision to paper because he couldn't see how he'd ever accomplish that when his life was already so busy. Now that he had it written down, he felt more committed than ever to doing whatever he could to make it happen. So he wrote down a specific goal—he wanted to have a third kid within the next two years. How he and his wife would find the time to devote to another child was not yet clear, but he wanted it enough that he would give his full attention to finding a way.

Remember, you were challenged to aim high and create a grand vision. In his book *Good to Great*, Jim Collins talks about the importance of setting "BHAGs"—big hairy audacious goals.[1] For a company, this is a high-reaching goal that reflects its peoples' passions, their ability to be the best, and something that will drive their economic engine. For you, audacious goals may also reflect your passions, tap your unique talents, and be something that will pay major dividends—such as bringing you joy, fulfillment, or financial rewards.

If you are like most people and organizations, you will have many more goals than you can tackle all at once. You will need a way to look at everything you'd like to accomplish so you can put first things first. It probably won't surprise you that, once again, the first step in that process is writing it all down so you can get a good visual of the *what* and *when*. Your custom closet holds the key—and your priorities.

Devise and Conquer

It's time to dig in and organize your thoughts. Here's how you will do it so you can get a well-rounded look at what matters most to you across some key areas. We've talked about the elusive balance that everyone seems to be seeking and not finding. The largest section of your custom closet is devoted to displaying your goals and priorities in a way that lets you visualize the balance you are emphasizing. Creating a clear picture will make it easier to see how to make it happen. There are two important dimensions to consider when setting and prioritizing your goals: *what* you want to do and *when* you want to do it.

WHAT You Want

One way to attack the challenge of deciding what your priorities should be is to set goals in each of four major areas:

- Family and relationships
- Career or vocation

- Community engagement/service
- Mind/body/spirit

Remember that this is a *custom* closet, so it is up to you how much emphasis you want to place on each of these areas. Balance is a function of *your* individual priorities.

WHEN You Want It

The second dimension you will consider is the time horizon. I happen to believe you can have it all—just not all at once. Nor would you want to, really. How can you be fully present to experience everything all at once? So, you will think about when you want to get to everything over time. Once again, you can customize your closet to reflect the time frames that make the most sense for you given the nature of your goals and their relationship to one another.

People often ask me about the "right" time frame for goal setting. The answer to that question always depends on the nature of your goals and your particular circumstances. The goal of curing cancer would obviously take a lot longer than finding retail space for your new bakery. Likewise, the goal of earning your MBA will take longer to achieve if you don't have your undergraduate degree than it would if you already have that credential.

As you consider your priorities, it's easiest to begin by thinking about what you want to accomplish right now. What do you need to do to fulfill the vision you've established for yourself? Do you have a good balance of activities across the many roles you play, given your current circumstances? Are you getting enough exercise? Sleep? What represents a good balance for you today may not be so relevant next year. If you're working full time and pursuing that MBA at night, your goal may just be to hold it all together until you earn your degree. A year from now, with classes behind you and a new credential, you may have very different goals. In fact, it's not unlikely that earning your degree is a short-term goal that you undertook in order to fulfill a longer-term ambition.

If you have small children at home, you may have some things you'd like to pursue once they go off to college. Or, if you're facing retirement, you may be looking forward to how that new phase of your life could be most satisfying. If your current circumstances won't last more than a few years, thinking in one- and five-year increments might make a lot of sense for you. This is particularly true if you need to do something in the short term to be ready to meet your long-term objectives.

On the other hand, you might have such consuming short-term goals that taking a long-range view is too overwhelming for you. Only you can determine the appropriate time frame for your own goal setting in this moment. You will have ample opportunities to review your goals and add to them as it makes sense for you to do so. Set long-term goals if they serve you. Just be sure to avoid being so rigidly attached to making them happen that you pursue them even if they no longer fit a few years down the road.

What Goal-Setting Looks Like

Let's take a look at Regina, a project manager in a large information technology operation, who took my Business of Life course offered through her employer. She had an eighteen-month-old baby girl, and just the mention of her name lit up Regina's face. Her career was thriving and, overall, things were going pretty well. Her major issue: she was overweight and exhausted. While she had a satisfying job and a family she adored, she experienced melancholy that sometimes bordered on despair. As she considered her priorities, she realized that, as is all too common with working mothers, she was ignoring her own health just to get through her epic daily to-do list. It was clear that she needed to put some emphasis on taking care of herself since her bouts of depression coincided with the ebbs in her energy level. Her goal-setting exercise made it very clear how she could accomplish this goal while meeting other key objectives at the same time.

REGINA'S PRIORITIES EXERCISE

	Family/ Relationships	Career/Vocation	Community	Mind/Body/ Spirit
Long Term (1–5 years)	Have a second child	Get promoted	Serve on a nonprofit board of directors	
Medium Term (within a year)		Take courses toward MBA offered by employer		
Short Term (now)	Date night with husband every other Saturday night Take baby for walk		Sing in church choir	Get to the gym 3x a week Take baby for walk other 4 days Sing in church choir

Regina was relieved to see her priorities seemed doable once they were laid out before her. She was happy to see that she could do things that brought her joy, met her family goals, and put her health in the mix. She vowed to get some physical activity daily and committed to getting to the gym three days a week. On her off days, she would take the baby for a walk. In that way, she could spend some time on her family priorities and get some exercise at the same time. Likewise, she loved to sing and decided to join her church choir. That gave her some much-needed connection to her community and built in time to attend to her spirit. Just seeing these few shifts boosted her morale and gave her hope that her health—and moods—would improve.

You're In Charge

I'd like to underscore the importance of this exercise reflecting *your own* priorities. It's very easy to get so caught up with people pleasing and other tendencies that you end up spending inordinate amounts of time on activities that don't really mean that much to you. This can be an insidious problem because we're often fooled by the way the invitation or request is framed. Like the time my nine-year-old niece told my sister-in-law, "It's Mother's Day. You can use whatever kind of fabric softener you want." Generous offer indeed, but who said she wanted to spend her special day indulging her laundry habit in the first place? So beware, this is one way to get pulled into doing someone else's bidding even if we're invited to do their thing our way.

The Goals of Goal Setting

A detailed list of goals acts as a ready reminder of your priorities and serves as a rudder that guides your investments to produce the best possible results given your current circumstances, while still taking the long view.

Decision-Making Filter

This tool worked so well for reordering my priorities when my son was born, after I'd spent my whole pregnancy wondering if he would survive birth. Thankfully, he did, but we weren't out of the woods. He had an unusual set of cardiac anomalies that required we keep close watch on him because sudden death was a lurking possibility for the first two years of his tender life. There was no question that family was my top, burning priority in those years. Community service, as important as it is to me, would have to wait until I saw my son through this critical time. Other people could support worthy causes, but only I could mother my son.

Once his condition no longer required such vigilance and I could do a limited amount of volunteer work, my priorities were clear. After facing the prospect of losing my precious child, I knew that as long as my children lived at home, family life was my absolute top priority and other decisions would be shaped by what was best for them. So as I added community service back into the mix, I had specific criteria for which projects I would accept. The organization requesting help would have to:

1. Benefit my children or family
2. Need a skill that I uniquely possessed
3. Require a time-limited commitment
4. Have a pleasant team capable of sustaining the value of our work

If those conditions were met, I would accept. If not, I would politely decline, saying I'd consider it once my kids moved on to college. Done. No guilt. No second-guessing myself.

Balance and Perspective

Many professionals I work with struggle with finding a good balance of work and personal life. Paul is no exception —except he had no awareness of his problem until he got to the goal-setting exercise in his Business of Life workshop. He'd signed up for the course because he had just relocated to Boston to take on a new position as finance manager in a large corporation. He felt that all he'd learned in his MBA program years earlier was a bit rusty, so he thought the class would be a good chance to brush up on his skills. He came expecting to focus on strategic planning and implementation techniques. But when he started filling in his priorities in his Custom Life Closet, he was slightly alarmed to see that he had put all of his attention on his career and he'd paid scant attention to any other aspects of his life. He was living in a new city where he didn't know anyone and had no connection to the community. What's more, he was so concerned about meeting the expectations of his new boss that he'd not focused much on his own health or recreation. This look in his closet was a big wake-up call.

Melissa is a manager who came to my Business of Life course hoping to find a way to be recognized by her vice president as the leader she was and to upgrade the status of her position to reflect that understanding. Achieving this goal would also affect her forty colleagues holding the same title. Almost as soon as her six-week course began, she realized that she had a number of additional areas to improve beyond work, and creating a business plan for her life was the key:

> The most important thing I learned from the class, what really turned things around for me, was setting long-term goals. I'd been a big fan of to-do lists and loved crossing completed tasks off my list. But I'd never really stepped back to think about what I wanted to accomplish over time. Changing the operations coordinators jobs to operations managers wouldn't have happened if we weren't able to take that longer-term view. Everything I'd done up until then was just responding to doing what needed to be done. Thinking about what I wanted to accomplish long term let me set goals and make strategies to accomplish them. That was big.

Taking the long view also allowed Melissa to see that just "going along to get along" was driving her to make decisions that were in conflict with her personal goals. She described it this way, "The closet also really helped me see I was putting all my effort into work and my personal life was suffering. So I used the same goal setting to accomplish personal goals as well. This made it possible for me to find balance between my office and home life."

Melissa's vision statement had her in her new position as an operations manager and working on mastering the art of managing other people. But her vision expanded well beyond work and included a vivid description of her joyful home life that included a husband and children. Until she started working on her priorities, she hadn't really thought much about how that was going to happen.

Many times we're doing something that keeps us from fulfilling our desires that is so obvious, but only once we stop to look at it in context. Yes, Melissa wanted to get married and build a family. But it wasn't until she looked at this goal with the intention of creating a plan to make it happen that she could see she was doing things that were not conducive to finding a husband. Not only was she focused almost entirely on her career, she had allowed her brother to move into her tiny apartment rent-free. With little free time and no privacy at home, it would be hard to find and nurture an intimate relationship with anyone else.

Within a year of developing her plan, she'd worked with the other operations coordinators to develop a forum where they could share challenges and best practices. I was delighted when she asked me to facilitate a retreat for this group and help them develop a strategy to get their positions upgraded, even at a time when her employer was facing layoffs and budget cuts. Melissa was fortunate that Jeanette, her senior vice president, had created an environment that encourages innovation from all the clinical and administrative staff and "supports their power to create positive change." Melissa's director, George, attended the retreat she organized. While the leadership needed to eliminate some positions, Melissa and her colleagues agreed to cover more units if their positions were upgraded to compensate for the additional work. That way, they would need fewer people and would save money while still getting all the work done. They found the win–win for her group and her department's leaders, and Melissa and her colleagues got the title and salary they so richly deserved.

With that success under her belt, she saw the power of setting specific goals. Thus emboldened, she turned her attention to her personal life. Melissa made a point of doing something every week where she might meet new people and she asked her brother to find another place to live. With a new focus and a bit of luck, it didn't take her long to meet and marry her husband. Their first child is due any day and she couldn't be happier.

Presence Leads to Pleasure

The hundreds of busy professionals I've taught and coached over the years share a common struggle: they try to do too much. High achievers think they can do it all. Often they can, but at a great cost to themselves.

A physician enrolled in the Business of Life course because she was feeling burned out from the emotional intensity of meeting her cancer patients' medical and personal needs while keeping up with the demands of her young family. She said of her experience:

> I came to this class feeling guilty trying to do it all and doing nothing well. Now I feel so empowered. You taught me to be present and fully commit to whatever it was I chose to do. Everything changed. I actually played trains with my son without folding laundry at the same time. And to my surprise, it was fun. Until recently, I haven't had much fun in my life.
>
> Even work has changed. I experience much more joy when I allow myself to be fully there for my patients and give them my undivided attention. It gives me great satisfaction to help my frightened patients face their disease with optimism. The tools you taught me allowed me to let go of worrying about all the trivial tasks that needed doing. Your advice to schedule time on the calendar to complete these tasks was so simple, yet so powerful.

All it took for this bright and talented woman to find some joy from all of the effort she was expending was setting a goal of doing so and shifting her focus enough to let it happen. She learned to let go of the unimportant to make room for what really mattered. And it took no time at all to accomplish that—just awareness.

Toolbox

Presence

Staying in the moment is a powerful tool for finding joy or at least fully experiencing whatever it is you choose to do. We miss out on a lot of pleasure when our minds are on anything but what we're doing in the moment. So when you choose to do something, commit to focusing on it and giving it your all—in that moment.

Choose and Commit

One thing that makes me exceptionally sad is hearing from new mothers who return to work after their maternity leave saying, "I didn't accomplish a thing." They had expected to paint the house, write the great American novel, or plant a new garden in their "time off." I ask them how many diapers they changed, how many times they fed and bathed their tiny new companion or kissed his sweet-smelling head. Their job was bonding with their baby and giving her a good start in life. And yet, they missed the fact that they had indeed accomplished what they'd really set out to do. Their wistful, in-retrospect smile breaks my heart every time. So please be conscious of what you've chosen to do and commit to it fully. Then savor the memory of those satisfying moments. Don't look back with regret.

I witnessed a poignant reminder of just how important committing to being present is to those around us during my son's seventh-grade soccer season. His teammate's father traveled routinely for business and seldom came to his games. He finally made it to the last game of the season and the boy triumphantly looked to the sidelines when he scored the winning goal. But he crumpled to the ground in a sobbing heap when his searching eyes found his father on the phone with his back to the field. It would have been better for him if his father hadn't come at all, since his expectations were raised and then his hopes dashed. If you choose to go to a soccer game, or your equivalent, commit to really *being* there and let other distractions wait. Especially if someone else is counting on you.

Claim Your Power

Once we determined that the main thing standing between Brenda and the management career she desired was the college degree she never pursued because she simply accepted her middle school teacher's inaccurate declaration that she had no aptitude for math, she was able to set specific goals that would set her up to fulfill her dream. "Earn a college degree" was her ultimate goal, but that was so large and lofty that Brenda was afraid to commit to it. So, we talked about what she felt she *could* tackle as a first step. She agreed to face her fear head-on and set an immediate goal of taking a math course at a local university the very next semester. She agreed that if she passed that course, she would commit to the longer-term goal of pursuing her bachelor's degree.

Success

Another compelling reason to commit your goals to paper is the simple fact that it works. A recent study by Dr. Gail Matthews at Dominican University of California confirmed that people who wrote down their goals and committed to giving regular updates to their friends were 33 percent more likely to accomplish them than people who simply thought about their objectives.[2] For years, I've been pairing participants in my workshops with a "buddy" when the course ends and instructing them to check in at regular intervals to see how the other is doing. The accountability and mutual support has really helped people stay committed to their goals, ensuring long-term dividends on the time they invested in creating their personal business plan.

Eliminate Anxiety

If you are like many people I work with, you carry a lot of details in your head and worry that you'll forget something critically important. By writing down your goals and referring to them frequently, you can let go of that concern. You can free up some valuable real estate in your brain for other important pursuits.

Clarity

Goal setting may also help to clarify how you can use your strengths to achieve your vision, sometimes in a most unexpected way. Remember Diane, the doctor who wanted to positively impact the practice of medicine nationally while maintaining her busy clinical practice and being available to her young children? How she would achieve this eluded her even as she listed her critical success factors. Conducting her SWOT analysis reminded her of the pleasure she got from thoroughly researching the issues related to prescribing narcotics in order to write a policy manual for her hospital's primary care department.

She enjoyed being an expert on the nuances of this delicate matter facing doctors across the nation, and she'd noted this as a major strength on her SWOT. She realized that her depth of knowledge and understanding was a strength that would be of value well beyond the walls of her own institution and which had the potential for widespread impact on her profession. She'd recorded the need for better prescribing guidelines as an opportunity to leverage her knowledge on the national stage and she set a goal of establishing herself as a recognized leader in this area within five years. She had the added goal of having family dinners at least five nights a week until her youngest child left for college in thirteen years. With her list of critical success factors and SWOT in hand, she set an immediate goal to turn a spare bedroom into her home office. She would use the laptop her husband had given her as her home computer. She made a priority of speaking to her division chief about rearranging her clinical schedule and she booked another coaching session to work on strategies to put the remaining two critical success factors in place: her communications platform and salary for the nonclinical time. You will see the strategies she developed in step 7.

SMART Goals

I'm often asked what makes a "good" goal. The goal that you'll work toward, the one you're committed to achieving and whose achievement is likely to bring you closer to fulfilling your vision is a good one. In management circles, the goals voted most likely to succeed are SMART:

- Specific
- Measureable
- Attainable
- Realistic
- Timely

So consider these attributes as you think about your own goals. A specific goal says "I will lose ten pounds by Christmas by exercising before work three times a week and cutting out sweets." This goal has a much higher likelihood of getting results than the more general "I want to lose weight," because it leads clearly to specific actions. Wishing doesn't make something so. And plenty of research bears this out. In her book *Succeed*,[3] Heidi Grant Halvorson describes an experiment conducted by German social psychologist Peter Gollwitzer that showed that students who planned the time and place that they would write their essays were more than twice as likely to complete them on time than those who simply agreed to write it over Christmas break.

Measurable goals can be tracked easily, and monitoring your progress can keep you motivated to keep moving forward. Watching those ten pounds melt away, one at a time, inspires continued vigilance.

Setting attainable and realistic goals is not the same as setting easy ones. You can still challenge yourself and aim high. Attainable means that you have the skills and capacities to make them happen—these are the strengths in your SWOT. Realistic means that you are willing and able to work toward it. If there's no way you'll give up your daily hot fudge sundae, losing ten pounds by giving up sweets is not a realistic goal for you.

Finally, time-bounded goals create a sense of urgency and get you moving. Losing those ten pounds by Christmas means you'd better get started with your exercise program now since that's right around the corner. Without that deadline, you can always start your regimen tomorrow. A tomorrow that never comes.

Melissa's goals were SMART. To meet her future husband, she set a goal of enrolling in an on-line dating service and meeting at least one new person a month (specific and measurable). She had plenty of friends who had done the same thing, so she knew this was attainable and realistic. She also planned to start immediately. It would be hard to be more timely than that.

Goal-Setting Guidelines

As you prepare to write down your own goals, here are a few points to consider.

- Remember that having it all is not the same as doing it all. So focus on what's most important. You will never be able to do everything, and accepting that simple fact can be liberating.
- Don't let fear inhibit your ambitions.
- Consider breaking large goals into smaller "mini goals." "Lose one hundred pounds" is such a big goal that it may seem undoable. "Join a gym" and "hire a nutrition coach" are actionable priorities that you can commit to and hold yourself accountable for achieving.
- Be sure to include "joy notes" and keep pleasure among your priorities. As Danielle, our soon-to-be-laid-off fashion buyer,

approached redefining her work life, she had a hard time knowing where to start. When she reviewed her self-assessment, she took note of how much she enjoyed cooking even though she hadn't done much of that while she was working and commuting such long hours. So, to prime her goal-setting pump, she put taking a cooking class on her list of short-term priorities just to inject some fun into her days. Little did she know where that decision would lead her a few months down the road.

EXERCISE

Set Your Goals and Priorities

Make your own version of a custom closet in your notebook or download one from joyofstrategy.com.

- Write down your goals and priorities across the four major areas: work/career, family/relationships, community, and mind/body/spirit. Check to see that you are happy with the distribution of your priorities and that they reflect your sense of a good balance among them.
- Consider your short-, medium-, and long-term goals. Those shelves are there for you if you find them helpful. You are under no obligation to fill them all with priorities. Recording long-term goals is especially helpful if you need to accomplish short-term goals to be ready when the time comes to fulfill the later objective. If you have the goal of flying around the world in ten years, you may want to set short-term goals that include getting your pilot's license and saving up to buy a plane.
- Be sure to include some health-related goals to make sure your body runs efficiently, so that you feel well and are capable of enjoying whatever it is you choose to do.
- Once you've recorded your priorities, color code each one as follows:

- ○ green = most important, highest priority
- ○ yellow = medium priority
- ○ red = least important, low priority

Consider why any low-priority items are on your list and think about eliminating them.

Your color-coded closet gives you a nice visual of how you want to spend your precious time and other resources. Take one more look at your priorities and goals. If you are able to accomplish everything, will you fulfill your mission and vision? Consider adding to your list until your answer to that question is a resounding "yes."

Toolbox

got joy?

As you set your goals and priorities, do a gut check and see how you feel about your choices. Do your goals excite you and inspire you to act? Do they tip your scale away from hassle toward joy? The goals that you are most likely to pursue fully are those that will bring you pleasure and fulfillment. Be sure to include a healthy dose of happiness among your priorities.

Step ❻

Perform a Time and Emotion Study

"How we spend our days, of course, is how we spend our lives."[1]

—Annie Dillard

Money can't buy me love and it can't buy more time either. Now that you have a closet full of goals, you may be wondering how you'll find time to do everything on your list. As I keep emphasizing, a strategic plan for your life requires being mindful about what you want to achieve in your heart of hearts and *deliberately* using your limited resources (time, money, energy, and attention) to get the results you want. For most of us, time is in especially short supply. No matter how wealthy you may be, you get the same twenty-four-hour days as everyone else, so you will need to manage this essential resource as carefully as possible.

In this step of the planning process, you will look at:

- How well your current use of time lines up with your newly stated goals
- What is contributing to any lack of alignment between your actions and priorities
- Tips and tools to clear the clutter and make room for what matters most to you

Diagnosis: Match Your Doings to Your Desires

You will start by conducting what I call a time and emotion study. It's as simple as taking a hard look at your calendar to see how you are currently investing your time compared to what you'd be doing if you were living in perfect harmony with the goals and priorities you just identified. Your emotions also give you valuable information about how well your actions are aligned with your mission, vision, and values, so you will pay attention to how you feel about what you see on your schedule.

This straightforward exercise will give you a great idea of what's working well for you and it will show you what you're doing that's robbing you of joy or standing in the way of your goals. Warning: your first look may be disheartening if you've fallen into some counterproductive habits. Remember that essential to fixing any problem is recognizing that it exists in the first place. Be gentle with yourself and view this as an opportunity to reclaim any time you are not using optimally and redirect it toward more worthy pursuits. While your calendar may feel like your enemy at the beginning of this step, you will turn it into a critical tool that serves your higher purpose in the end. So just be curious and see what possibilities present themselves. This simple exercise normally takes less than thirty minutes to complete, and many people I know have found several hours they could free up each week: not a bad return on investment.

EXERCISE

Time and Emotion Study: How Do You Spend Your Time?

Part One: Complete Your Calendar
For this exercise, you will recreate your calendar, formatted to line up with the section of your custom closet that contains your goals and priorities. Start by looking at how you spend a typical day. I know;

there rarely is a "typical" day. Just do your best. Usually, it makes the most sense to start by looking at a workday. Then you can use a weekly view and/or a monthly view to factor in weekends and occasional activities. For example, you buy groceries every Saturday and you volunteer at a soup kitchen the second Sunday of the month.

Record how you're using all of your time, and slot each activity into one of the four categories you assigned to your goals. Just choose the one that fits best. The more specifically and completely you record *all* of your actions, no matter how trivial, the more information you will have to work with. How you assign an activity may depend on why you do it and what you expect to get from it. For example, watching television may fit best into mind/body/spirit if you zone out in front of the tube by yourself every night. However, viewing a televised presidential debate may be a family/relationship activity if you're watching with your kids so you can discuss its impact on world events later.

After you've filled in your calendar, grab the same markers you used in assigning priority scores to your goals and do the same thing for your current activities. Highlight your most important actions in green, use yellow for moderately important activities, and use red for the least important ones. Then mark each with asterisks to denote its level of urgency: three stars go to the most urgent, two to the moderately urgent, and one for less urgent or long-term activities. In the TV example, tuning in for half an hour to decompress from the workday so you can transition to your evening activities may fit best in mind/body/spirit. It works well and gives you some "me" time, so you might color it yellow or even green and assign it two or three stars. But if you don't find that it actually refreshes you, or half an hour turns into an entire mindless evening, you may highlight it in red and give it one star. Alternatively, the presidential debate contributes to family time well spent and informs you all about community matters. That may earn it a green rating. And it's certainly urgent when preparing you to vote responsibly and discuss current events at work or school the next day. That earns it three stars. Here's an example of what your calendar shell might look like.

DAILY SCHEDULE

	Family/ Relationships	Career/Vocation	Community	Mind/Body/ Spirit
AM				
5:00				
6:00				
7:00				
8:00				
9:00				
10:00				
11:00				
PM				
12:00				
1:00				
2:00				
3:00				
4:00				
5:00				
6:00				
7:00				
8:00				
9:00				
10:00				
11:00				

Part Two: Analyze Your Agenda

To assess how you are using your time, hold your color-coded calendar next to your color-coded goals and priorities. How similar do they look? Are any glaring differences immediately apparent? Be careful not to judge yourself too harshly if the images do not line up as well as you might like. For one thing, you just did a lot of work to set your goals and order your priorities, so it would be surprising if they were already perfect reflections of one another.

To help zero in on where your issues are and where opportunities present themselves, answer the guiding questions below. Consider where you might be able to make some adjustments and write that down in your notebook.

TIME SPENT ON PRIORITIES
- How much time am I spending on my most important/urgent activities?
- Am I devoting enough attention to make progress on each of my important goals?
- Are any priorities missing from my calendar?
- Am I preparing to address longer-term priorities?
- What am I doing that isn't on my list of priorities? Does it merit my time?
- Do I have time to accommodate everything I want to do?

HARMONY: ALIGNMENT OF ACTIONS AND ASPIRATIONS
- How do I spend my time?
- Am I using my unique skills and talents?
- Are my actions in harmony with my core values? Mission? Vision?

MISSPENT TIME
- What am I spending time on that is *not* important to me?
- *Why* am I spending time on non-value-added activities?
- What am I not getting to because I'm spending time on unimportant matters?

How Do You Feel About Your Calendar?

It's about this time in my workshops that the business planning process gets very real for some people, especially those who tend to be more task-oriented. That's because the earlier steps were all about getting clear and about what you want and setting some goals to help you get it. At this point, people start to see very concretely how what they do day to day is either helping or hindering their progress. Some discover they are on the right track. They may need only minor tweaks to their schedules to be able to attend to everything they value. Others, not so much. If you feel a groan of your own rising in your throat, fear not. You are now going to look at why you do the things you do and how you can make some needed adjustments so your actions are more in harmony with your goals. Remember, this is not about passing judgment or berating yourself if you've made some subpar choices in the past. Consider this a simple diagnostic exercise that will lead you to some effective treatments. Here are some common discoveries people made during this exercise and what they did about them.

Scale Tilts Hard Toward the Left

It is quite common for professionals, particularly those who are raising young children, to see lots of activities in the career and family sections and precious little in community and mind/body/spirit. The daily demands placed on us by our families and employers often consume every waking moment. The first thing to give is often our own self-care—sufficient sleep, exercise, and leisure time. Yet neglecting our health in favor of investing more time in other areas can paradoxically lead us to be *less* effective in these pursuits. It's hard to be attentive in a meeting if you aren't feeling your best, for one example.

When Regina, the IT project manager who set some new goals in the last chapter, reviewed her calendar, it revealed what she already knew. She put all of her time into work and family and paid the price with her rising weight and falling spirits. While she liked her work and cherished her husband and young child, she was less and less able to enjoy them. Failing to get enough sleep day after day, she tried to boost her flagging energy with coffee and sweets. Not only did she not lose the weight she'd put on during her pregnancy, she'd gained another thirty pounds in the eighteen months since her daughter was born.

She was not surprised when her calendar revealed that she spent no time exercising and relied on fast food dinners far too often to be healthy. Her husband worked later hours and when he wasn't home for dinner, she grabbed whatever she could for dinner and ate while watching whatever was on television. She was embarrassed to realize when she filled out her calendar how many full evenings she spent snacking and zoning out in front of the TV until she finally dragged herself to bed. It was easy to see why she'd put on so much weight. She was just so tired at the end of the day there was no energy left for anything else.

However, she was especially troubled by the realization that she was teaching her daughter some very bad habits. She resolved in that moment to add exercise to her schedule and to do some of it with her daughter. She joined the gym at her company and planned to spend her lunch hour working out three days a week. By taking walks with her daughter on the days she didn't get to the gym, she was able to meet her goal of exercising daily without compromising family time. In fact, she was happy to be modeling healthy behavior for her daughter.

Regina was so motivated to improve her eating and exercise habits that she decided it was worth it to let her daughter eat a little later two evenings a week so they could go for a walk before they settled down for the evening. They also walked both days on weekends and Regina was surprised how much she enjoyed her exercise regime. Her daughter enjoyed being outside, and evenings were much more peaceful when they returned. Regina was also happily amazed that she had much more energy when she walked in the evenings. When she wasn't so tired, it was easier to make the effort to cook something healthy for dinner. As the pounds slowly dropped, she felt better and better. Eventually, she felt well enough in the evenings to do more than collapse in front of the TV. These small changes required very little tweaking to her calendar. Small changes created a huge shift in

REGINA'S DAILY SCHEDULE

	Relationships	Career/ Vocation	Mind/Body/ Spirit	Community
AM				
5:00			Sleep	
6:00	Feed baby, prepare for day			
7:00		Commute		
8:00		Work		
9:00		Work		
10:00		Work		
11:00		Work		
12:00		Work/Lunch		
PM				
1:00		Work		
2:00		Work		
3:00		Work		
4:00		Work		
5:00		Commute		
6:00	Feed baby			
7:00	Family time to play/read, put baby to bed			
8:00			Dinner/Watch TV	
9:00			Snack/Watch TV	
10:00			Watch TV Sleep	
11:00			Sleep	

her health and mood. She felt more equipped to start preparing for some of her longer-term goals.

With their schedules somewhat out of sync during the week, Regina and her husband had to make a special effort to spend time together on the weekends. She had set an immediate goal of having a date night every other Saturday. To her delight, her husband suggested they go out every Saturday. She felt that her improved moods made her better company, so he was more excited about spending time with her. She was even more thrilled when her niece agreed to babysit every week.

Regina was able to accomplish her community goals at church on the weekends. She reported back to me that she's been able to maintain and even improve on her new habits for the past several years and has just started a part-time MBA program and takes classes two evenings a week. She credits her improved eating and exercise habits for making that possible. And those big changes required only a slight shift on her schedule.

Not Having Such a Wonderful Time, Wish I Were Here

Thelma had a tougher challenge when she looked at her calendar next to her goals and priorities. She was nowhere to be found in either place. She had focused a great deal of effort on her career and she was thriving at work. It wasn't until she was discussing her goals and strategies in her Business of Life workshop that she realized just how absent she had been from her own priorities, let alone her agenda. She spent virtually no time attending to her personal needs that included exercise and some kind of spiritual practice.

She was seeking input from the class on her goal to stop yelling at her husband and son so much. She yearned to enjoy their family time, but found that what little they had was often filled with tension and discord. The men in her life continuously dropped their socks on the living room floor and left their clothes all over the house despite her constant (loud) requests that they put their things away. Her classmates were not impressed with her proposed strategy—rather than continuing to scold her husband and son, going forward, she intended to bite her tongue every time she saw the offending laundry and just pick it up and put it away. They told Thelma that not only would she have some nasty teeth marks, keeping her mouth shut would lead to simmering resentment that was likely to come to a boil over time. Her colleagues pointed out that her proposed approach would only continue to train her husband and son that it was okay with her that they disregarded her feelings and were as slovenly as they pleased.

What was so obvious to everyone else was a revelation to Thelma, who was used to being a highly regarded and effective leader at work. She was truly stunned to confront what she tolerated at home. One more look at her goals and calendar confirmed that she needed to make herself a priority.

Thelma's calendar revealed that she spent at least an hour each day on housework. Despite the fact that she had a husband and two able-bodied teens in the house, she carried most of this responsibility on her own shoulders. She put a load of wash in before work and dried and folded it in the evenings. It was no wonder that she was so angry with her husband and son when they dropped their socks on the floor even as she folded the laundry. Now that she confronted the reality of her situation while she discussed its implications with her classmates, she was even angrier with herself for letting it go on for so long. She also faced up to the fact that all her yelling wasn't changing their behavior. There had to be a better approach.

She had been intrigued and somewhat disquieted by the discussion in class about the importance of being present and decided to set some goals to cultivate awareness in that area. She realized she didn't feel as connected to her kids, especially her son, as she'd like to be. Upon reflection, she thought she could make more of an effort to focus on him, his schoolwork, his social life, and just having some fun with him. It would lighten the mood around the house and maybe open up an opportunity to talk about some things that mattered to her. She thought she'd have more success getting through to him if she could talk to him calmly when she wasn't angrily picking up his socks.

Thelma had long been frustrated by the time she felt was wasted in meetings and commuting, but it wasn't until she did her time and emotion study that she made a serious effort to make some changes. And those shifts were profound.

Thelma's staff worked in a few different locations. Once she established strong relationships, she held more of their regular meetings by phone, saving precious travel time in between. She also reduced the time she allotted to most meetings to thirty minutes rather than the hour she'd defaulted to in the past more out of habit than necessity. She also started to schedule conferences she could conduct by phone or remote meeting software at the beginning and end of the workday so she could participate from home. That allowed her to commute outside of rush hour, saving as much as ninety minutes in travel time and avoiding maddening frustration. As important, she was able to see her son off to school in the mornings and be home earlier in the evenings. A special bonus—she found she was much more patient and able to focus her full attention on him when she wasn't so worn out and stressed by her commute.

Now that she was close to home some mornings, she could get up early, go to a six a.m. yoga class (for exercise and meditation, a nice "twofer") and be back home to see her kids before starting her meetings. She has found that her days are more pleasant and productive when they start off that way.

By making these small shifts, her mornings and evenings went much more smoothly and efficiently. She got more done in less time and created precious space to think and plan. And she did so just in time since, little did she know, her home life was about to hit the fan. We'll see what happened and what she did about it later in the book.

We Just Keep Adding to the List

Bruce is the mid-level manager who, along with his wife, had a vision that included having a third child. This busy two-career couple couldn't see how they could possibly make time for more offspring. Until, that is, Bruce made an important discovery when reviewing his time and emotion study. Bruce and Mara had worked long hours for years as they established their careers and were quite satisfied with their progress. Bruce's calendar revealed some inertia and a pattern of working extraordinarily long hours that persisted longer than was necessary. He and Mara had agreed when they were newly married that they would work hard and advance professionally before having kids. They had their children right on schedule, but they'd forgotten an important part of their plan.

They'd never scaled back their work hours, though their careers were long past the point when they needed to put in extra hours to prove themselves on the job. Like many professionals, they excelled at adding new activities to their calendars but were remiss in removing old ones that no longer served an important purpose. Bruce knew in the early years of his management career that he would have to put in a lot of "face time" to establish his credibility, reputation, and relationships. That goal was accomplished years ago, but he had not made any adjustments to reflect his evolving status. As he reviewed his time and emotion study, he realized he no longer needed to serve on so many committees. And since he worked with surgeons, most of those meetings were held before and after normal business hours. Using a critical eye to determine which meetings were still necessary for him to attend, he determined that he could step down from three working groups. Doing so would free up two evenings and one morning a week.

After Bruce stepped down from those extra committees, he was able to have dinner with his family four nights a week. On the morning that was freed up, Bruce stayed home and made breakfast for the kids. He also skipped the gym that day so Mara could get in a workout for herself. Each week, Bruce whipped up French toast with a surprise topping and the kids took bets on what it would be. Thursday's breakfast turned into a much-anticipated ritual. Bruce also realized that, over time, he could adjust his work schedule further and start going into the office later most mornings.

What are you doing just because it hasn't occurred to you that it's

BRUCE'S DAILY SCHEDULE

	Relationships	Career/Vocation	Mind/Body/Spirit	Community
AM				
5:00			Arise and travel	
6:00		Work (2-3 days/week)	Exercise at gym 2-3 days	
7:00		Work		
8:00		Work		
9:00		Work		
10:00		Work		
11:00		Work		
12:00		Work		
PM				
1:00		Work		
2:00		Work		
3:00		Work		
4:00		Work		
5:00		Work		
6:00		Work		
7:00	Family dinner	Work (3 nights/wk)		
8:00	Bedtime routine			
9:00		Business reading, return e-mails		
10:00	Check in with Mara		Sleep	
11:00			Sleep	

no longer important for you to be doing it? For me, that was getting my eight-year-old son his milk every time he wanted a drink. For some reason, I hadn't noticed he'd long since been able to reach the milk and glasses just as well as I could. At some point, our children can switch from being a cost center to a revenue center and they can actually be some help around the house. We just have to remember to ask them.

I've Left Joy off My Agenda

Using our time well is essential to our sense of well-being. Feeling fulfilled requires putting our talents and passions to good use. As Aristotle said some 2,300 years ago, "we can't be truly happy unless and until we apply the fruits of our personal self-development to meeting the needs of others."[2]

Danielle, the fashion buyer who'd been stuck in a career she hated for twenty years, saw an opportunity to add more fun to her schedule immediately, even while she took time to find a new career direction. She'd set a goal of taking a cooking class because she enjoyed being in the kitchen so much. She also loved cooking for her husband, delighting him with artistically presented delicacies, so she set a goal of doing that at least once a week. She got such a boost from his obvious enjoyment of her cooking that she ended up preparing elaborate meals even more frequently. Between the delicious cuisine and the special time she had with her husband, every dinner felt like a celebration.

Get to the Heart of the Matter

If you find yourself relating to any of these dilemmas or have identified some other patterns of your own, there is plenty you can do about it. Take another look at your calendar and consider the following:

- What are you doing that doesn't serve you well?
- Why are you doing it?
- What can you do to change it?
- What are you not doing that you'd like to add into the mix?

Allow yourself to be present with whatever is happening. Aim for understanding why you're in this situation and try not to judge yourself harshly.

Why Am I Doing What I'm Doing?

It's important to recognize what's driving your behavior so you can address the source of the problem rather than just the symptoms. Toyota developed a simple approach to root cause analysis that has since become quite popular in health care and other industries: the five whys. I've often employed this technique myself when leading large projects. And it also works well with my students and clients. Manufacturing leaders at Toyota found that if they asked the question "Why?" five times, they could get to the root of just about any problem.

Here's how it worked for one of my coaching clients who had a goal of exercising daily, but was having trouble finding the time to do so:

Why don't I work out every day?
I don't have enough time.

Why (don't I have enough time)?
My commute is taking longer than it used to.

Why (is my commute taking longer than it used to)?
I am driving instead of taking the train. Traffic is lousy.

Why (am I driving instead of taking the train)?
So my car is with me at the end of the day.

Why (do I need my car at the end of the day)?
So I can drive to the gym to exercise.

This gentleman discovered that, ironically, his strategy for exercising was the very thing that was preventing him from doing so. He changed strategies and bought a treadmill and a set of free weights. The clincher was that he convinced his wife that he "needed" a new flat-screen television and a DVR so he could record his favorite sporting events so that he always had something to watch when it was time to exercise. It worked so well that they added an elliptical machine to their home gym and started recording movies so they could work out together while watching something they both enjoyed. Problem solved.

> ### *Root Cause Analysis: Five Whys*
>
> Seek to find the cause of your problem so you can address it at its root rather than just treating the symptom. This gives you insight into what's leading to your dilemma and will help you find solutions that will have a lasting impact.

Is Fear at the Root of Any Misalignment?

Go back to your SWOT analysis. Did you identify with any of the fear-based behavioral patterns described in that chapter? Several of these can lead to spending time doing things that divert you from your priorities. Let's examine how some of these can suck precious time from your days.

- **People pleasing:** Fear of disappointing others can often lead you to do whatever they ask of you, even when you'd rather not. People with this problem have a very hard time saying "no" to all kinds of requests. If you find yourself volunteering for every extra project at work or bake sale at your church, consider carefully what it is costing you to do so. Ask yourself what would happen if you said no to one request. You might be surprised that often the answer is "very little."

- **Perfectionism:** Do you find that you are never satisfied with your work to the point that you continue revising it long after you've crossed the point of diminishing returns? Believe me, this is something I can relate to very well. This book is partially a product of that tendency. In fact, there's a good chance I'll redraft this very section next time I reread it.

As the famous "they" say, don't let perfect be the enemy of good. Many times, good is good enough. Save the extra effort for those initiatives that truly call for excellence. In management circles, we often work by the Pareto Principle, which states that 80 percent of the work on any given project is completed with the first 20 percent of effort. The return on the investment of that last 80 percent is far lower than the initial 20. Consider that tenet next time you're grinding away on trying to get something "perfect." I just did.

- **Control issues:** Controlling people are sure that no one else can do anything as well as they can, so they end up doing most everything themselves. These people often make lousy bosses because they either refuse to delegate anything or they second-guess everything they assign to others. If you fall prey to this belief, once again, consider what it is costing you. Doing things that others can accomplish reasonably well takes you away from other activities—perhaps even those where you really *are* the best one for the job. If you are a manager, your job is to coach your people so they can learn to be as good as, if not better than, you are at performing their tasks. Try a new approach. See if coaching your staff pays dividends in freed-up time for you to invest elsewhere.

- **Procrastination:** Despite Mark Twain's advice, "Never put off till tomorrow what can be put off till day-after-tomorrow just as well,"[3] chronic procrastinators waste a lot of time. And it's getting easier than ever to procrastinate when, with the stroke of a computer key, you can peek at your e-mail, satisfy even the most frivolous curiosity by looking up the price of sugar in Siberia on the Internet, or play just one more game of.... The digital age is shortening our attention spans and along with our attention goes the ability to complete a task efficiently and effectively. Mr. Twain's wry observation may actually help determine the urgency of a given task and guide us to make a good decision about when to accomplish it. And taking scheduled breaks to clear your mind and refresh yourself may boost productivity. But protracted procrastination can prevent you from achieving a goal. Take an honest look at your calendar—make sure you've accurately filled in how you *really* spend your time. Do you find evidence of chronic procrastination?

Find Some Fixes

Now that you've examined what's driving your behavior, you can address any tendencies that are working against you. The following are a few more time management ideas. In the next chapter, you will learn a whole array of tools you can employ to choose those strategies that optimize your chances for success.

Tame the Electronic Beast

By far, the single thing that robs my clients, colleagues, and kids of precious time are the never-ending, ever-growing options for distracting ourselves with computer games, e-mail, texting, social media, podcasts, and on and on. The information age has many of us feeling like we are hopelessly behind in our knowledge because no human being can possibly keep up with the constant barrage of really cool stuff coming our way. And I mean that sincerely. There *is* great information to be consumed. There are awesome games to be played. There's nothing wrong with much of what's out there. It's the sheer amount that is constantly and readily available to us that threatens our productivity.

These distractions impact more than just how much we get done. Dr. Glenn Wilson, a psychiatrist at King's College London, found that the IQ of workers who tried to juggle phone, texts, and e-mail messages fell by ten points, which is equivalent to missing a whole night's sleep and more than twice the decline seen after smoking marijuana.[4]

The lure is seductive, so we need to impose some discipline. Here are some techniques that have helped my clients.

• **Be mindful about your electronics use:** Make deliberate decisions about how much time you will allocate to these activities. This may sound simplistic, but having a plan puts you in control of how you use your time and makes you less likely to get swept away for too long.

• **Schedule breaks:** Big projects like writing a book, for instance, require long stretches of intense concentration that can be very difficult to sustain. It's easy to convince yourself that you "need" to take a quick look at your e-mail just to keep up. The problem is that quick peek often turns into an hour or more and it breaks your focus. One way to deal with this is to divide your work time into chunks that are punctuated with refreshing breaks. It's good to get up and move around. There is evidence that students perform better at school when bouts of physical activity are sprinkled throughout the day. Schedule time to look at e-mail, play a game, or surf the web, and discipline yourself to limit your break to the allotted time. It may help to know another respite is only ninety minutes away.

• **Beat your e-mail addiction:** Are you, like many of my clients, addicted to e-mail? Do you drop whatever you're doing the instant you hear the ping announcing yet another not-so-special delivery? I was on a wilderness hike out West with a friend who stopped every few minutes to pull his smartphone out of his pocket to see what juicy nugget just arrived. Really? I'm not sure which is worse—that or the fact that nearly 40 percent of people admit to using their smartphones in the bathroom.

If your e-mail habit is distracting you, here is some advice:

○ Schedule two times a day to check and answer e-mail, and stay away from it at all other times.

○ Turn off alerts that let you know every time a message comes in.

○ Inform everyone that you will be checking your e-mails at the appointed times and will get back to them then. Putting a message on your out of office reply is a good way to do that. You can also let people know if they need a quicker response that they should contact you another way. Over time, people will learn what to expect from you and will adjust their behavior accordingly.

Put First Things First

Be mindful that your calendar reflects your priorities, and make conscious, well-considered choices about what is worthy of your time and attention. Use your mission, vision, and goals as filters that help you decide what you will do. Remember there are some things only you can do. Be sure to reserve time for the most essential items. For everything else, apply the "three D's" and ask yourself what can be:

• **Ditched:** Does each task need to be done? Ask yourself what would happen if it wasn't completed. If there isn't a serious consequence, consider dropping it from your list.

• **Delegated:** Okay, so it has to be done, but does it have to be done by you? Is there someone else who could handle this task?

• **Delayed:** How urgent is this task? When is the most appropriate time to tackle it, considering everything else on your list?

Put Last Things off the List

Many of us live by our to-do lists, but few of us have mastered the "not-to-do" list. This is not the same as not getting to something on the to-do list. This is about deliberately choosing *not* to do something that will not yield much value. If you have lots of red on your calendar, this may be an especially fruitful exercise for you. Ask yourself why you are doing things that have limited utility and consider eliminating them.

Toolbox

Not-To-Do List

Before you schedule every activity someone requests of you, take a moment to consider carefully whether it merits the time it would require. It's easier to be judicious before adding something to your load than it is to back out later once people are counting on you.

"There is more to life than simply increasing its speed."[5]

—Mahatma Gandhi

Remember that one reason for creating a business plan for your life is to be present and get the full value from whatever it is you choose to do. Trying to cram too much activity into a crowded schedule is not a great recipe for staying in the moment. So do give careful consideration to using the not-to-do list as another way to avoid letting unimportant things creep onto your calendar.

Once you've convinced yourself that everything on your calendar deserves its place, you will want to be sure you're as efficient as possible. There are many excellent books on time management that offer detailed approaches to improving productivity. David Allen's *Getting Things Done: The Art of Stress-Free Productivity*,[6] offers a thoughtful system that you may want to consider reviewing.

Toolbox

Calendar

If you are prone to distractions, use your calendar to schedule time to enjoy activities that might otherwise sidetrack you from the task at hand. Allow yourself a certain amount of time for breaks a few times a day when you can indulge these diversions. Be disciplined and stick within the allotted time. Then return to your task with new focus.

Frequently interrupted? Schedule office hours and tell your colleagues or students to come during the appointed time only.

If you struggle with perfectionism, schedule a specific amount of time for a given undertaking. Factor in a set number of inputs and revisions and then resolve to be satisfied with the result.

When your actions are guided by your core beliefs and you're focused on priorities that you've chosen consciously, you'll feel balanced. Purposeful. Joyful. And you'll keep heading steadily in the direction of fulfilling your vision. Hopefully you now have that wonderful sense of order and possibility that comes from cleaning all the old junk out of your closet. With room to breathe, you can contemplate how best to invest your newfound time to achieve your goals. In the next step, you will develop some strategies to do just that.

Step **7**

Select Successful Strategies:
Tools to Set You on a Productive Path

"Action expresses priorities."

—Mahatma Gandhi

Designing a business plan for your life is all about setting you up to live with integrity—so that what you do is a true reflection of who you are and what you value. In this step, you will select the strategies that best serve your priorities and are most likely to bring your glowing vision to life. You will get very specific about *how* you will accomplish those objectives. Sometimes the approach is fairly obvious—it's almost a given. If your goal is to have Sunday brunch with the family every week, you probably don't have to create overwrought plans to do that. You all love pancakes and orange juice and sleeping in. So you decide to meet at the table by eleven, agree to rotate cooking and grocery shopping duties, and you're pretty much there. For more complex goals, however, such as switching careers or pursuing a promotion, you will need a more sophisticated plan. In this section, you will sift through your potential strategies and choose those that are most likely to get you the results you desire.

To make wise choices, you will need to size up the alternatives and select the strategy that is most feasible and likely to work. And if previous efforts you've made to accomplish a goal have fallen short, you'll want to examine those as well, so you learn from your experiences and pick a more rewarding path. Bringing a vision to life takes skill.

This chapter offers a collection of tools you can use to evaluate your options, whether you seek to embark on a major life change or to simply make each day joyful and productive.

Jargon Alert

Are you finding yourself questioning what's a goal and what's a strategy? Wondering about the difference between priorities and objectives? Strategies and tactics? Don't worry about the terminology. Some business types spend a lot of time arguing over the lingo used to describe the strategic planning process. The names are not important. What matters is that you know *what* you want to do and *how* you will do it. You set goals and priorities so you are clear about *what* is most important for you to accomplish. This chapter is devoted to figuring out how you will get it done.

Here's one example of how people get tied up in knots. Say you've set a goal to lose ten pounds. Your strategy—the way you're going to accomplish that goal—is to cut refined sugar out of your diet and start an exercise program. Your exercise program could be accomplished with any number of tactics: join a gym, go for daily walks, ride a bike, and on and on. This chapter will help you decide which approach to the exercise program is most likely to lead you to success with your goal of losing weight.

Another person, however, might call starting an exercise program her goal. Maybe that contributes to a larger goal, such as "getting healthy." Or maybe exercise *is* the goal. That person will still need to get specific about how she is going to initiate her fitness regimen. So, one person may consider exercising a goal while the other thinks of it as a strategy to achieve a different goal. For one, the different exercise options are tactics while the other considers them strategies. Does it really matter?

For our purposes, we will use the term "strategy" to describe how you will accomplish something. Generally speaking, strategies are the general approach you will take and tactics are the smaller steps that contribute to the execution of a given strategy. There, you have the definitions if that helps you.

Make Sure Your List Is Complete

Before launching into action, let's be sure you are looking at the whole picture. Pull out your notebook. Review your mission and vision statements, both for inspiration and to ensure you've covered all your bases. Do you have all your critical success factors in place or a strategy to secure them?

Reviewing your critical success factors can serve as a good starting point for developing a winning strategy. Dr. Vicki Jackson is the director of Palliative Care at Massachusetts General Hospital and she successfully employed this technique as we worked on her department's strategic plan. To zero in on their priorities, we started with a look at their critical success factors. Vicki knows that the quality of the service she can provide is entirely dependent on employing the best practitioners in this young field, and she's been extraordinarily successful in this regard. A quality staff is her most essential success factor, so recruiting, retaining, and developing the best of the best is one of her top goals.

Her SWOT (strengths, weaknesses, opportunities, and threats) analysis showed her what she already knew. One of her division's greatest strengths is her highly dedicated and skilled multidisciplinary team of professionals. She knows not to take this extraordinary asset for granted as her profession faces serious threats nationally. First, the intense nature of their work with gravely ill patients, while richly rewarding, can be emotionally draining. Burnout is a well-known occupational hazard. Furthermore, there is an undersupply of qualified practitioners because the field is so new, so replacing her staff would not be a simple undertaking. Vicki intuitively understands that nurturing her clinicians' career growth and general well-being is essential to meeting her retention goal. As director, it is her responsibility to steward her resources wisely. She considers paying attention to how her people think *and* feel to be essential to the team's collective responsibility for managing their energy and emotions. This isn't a luxury in the palliative care field. It's a pragmatic necessity.

She also knows from experience that there is no "one size fits all" prescription for keeping everyone on the staff energized, so it is essential for her to offer an array of choices to address everyone's needs. Her approach, fittingly, was to appoint a task force led by two clinicians to develop a menu of renewal options. She calls this their sustainability strategy. While she respects the personal nature of this undertaking and doesn't dictate a single approach, she does insist that everyone on her team engage in some form of self-care to stave off burnout.

As you can see from this example, a significant part of the MGH palliative care strategy emerged directly from a review of the department's critical success factors, taking into account their strengths and weakness and evaluating the opportunities and threats presented by the state of their profession on the national level. As you review your strategic options, you will benefit from doing a similar analysis for yourself.

So Much to Do, So Little Time

You have a full life and are busy, busy. Most of what you're doing may even be pretty rewarding. As if that's not enough, you've just written down a closetful of goals to do even more. Your cup runneth over, but so doth your plate. There is far more on your list than you can possibly do. So how do you choose? In the last chapter, you reviewed your calendar and did some work to clear out the clutter. Now you can employ some new tools to judiciously determine what you add back to your schedule so that everything on it serves your goals and priorities.

Since you want your efforts to be both efficient and effective, this would be a good time to review your SWOT analysis. You need to ensure that your strategies leverage your strengths and opportunities, and that you have plans to address any potential weaknesses or threats. Remember not to get down on yourself for anything you've identified as a weakness. We all have them. Simple acceptance of the facts will allow you to think calmly about how to fill in for what you lack. From a resource-management perspective, you are far better off leveraging your strengths than trying to get up to speed to do everything yourself. If you happen to be lousy at math, all the math training in the world is likely to get you to adequate at best. And most of us are after excellent. So embrace your gifts and accept your limitations with grace and humility. Then go about finding other ways to fill in for your weaknesses if those points are necessary to achieving your goals.

Peggy and Gail are the artists who were starting Our Space, an organization to provide art therapy and other support for children affected by cancer. When they evaluated their readiness to launch this initiative, their SWOT, presented in step 4, revealed a mixed picture. They had a lot going for them, but their list of weaknesses showed that several of their critical success factors were not exactly in their wheelhouse. Their gap analysis revealed a significant lack of business know-how. They are very bright women, and certainly could have compensated for this particular weakness with courses at a local university. However, that would have taken years, and increasing their business education played neither to their strengths nor their passions. In one of their coaching sessions, we determined that there was likely a more expedient way to acquire the business acumen they needed, so we generated a list of alternate possibilities. You will see how they met this objective in the final chapter.

Admittedly, launching an entire organization is a complicated undertaking. So let's look at someone who had more modest goals. Mark is an attorney I coached who saw mixed results when he looked at his time and emotion study. He'd recently made partner at his firm after a concerted campaign to accomplish this long-term goal. He felt great about his achievement. However, his singular focus on work over the years took its toll. He had stopped his already sporadic exercise "program" in order to put in additional time on the job and had given up any semblance of a social life. His last physical revealed that his weight and blood pressure had started to creep up. He was interested in getting married and starting a family, but had not made much effort to go on dates or participate in any activities where he might meet his future bride. He had not contributed to any community service initiatives in recent memory and didn't feel so great about that.

A natural list maker, Mark started by brainstorming all of the ways he could fill in the gaps. Work was on a positive track, so focusing on the other three areas, he came up with something that looked like this:

Exercise	Social Life	Community Service
Run before work	Run with friends/family	Participate in events sponsored by his law firm
Join a gym	Invite someone to dinner out two nights a week	Raise money for children with autism
Trek the Himalayas	Join a hiking club	
Play tennis	Play tennis with friends	
Build a home gym	Ask friends to set him up on dates	

Even though Mark's time was still in pretty short supply, he decided to make daily exercise and reconnecting with friends and family immediate priorities. Being naturally very efficient in his actions, he looked for activities that could address one or more of his objectives at the same time. Running and playing tennis were two ways to improve his fitness that he could do with friends. That would help his social life as well. He'd always wanted to go trekking in Nepal. He thought joining a local hiking club might be a way to get in shape for a big trip and meet health-conscious women. He thought joining a gym might be another way to get fit and meet women. While he felt slightly less urgency to be active in community service, he looked for a convenient way to contribute to a cause that was personally meaningful and important to him. His nephew's struggles with autism touched him deeply and he hoped to find a way to make a difference for other families coping with this condition.

Despite the efficiencies he built into his list, he was still overwhelmed at the thought of adding more to his already crowded schedule. He just didn't know where to begin. So we used one of his coaching sessions to run his options through a series of tools and filters to zero in on the few things he *could* do that were most likely to achieve his larger goals of gaining better balance in his life and getting back into decent physical shape. As you will see illustrated below, when Mark used a series of tools to rank his priorities and multiply efficiencies, he began to reshape his schedule and take control of his life.

First Things First: Prioritization Tools

When the demands for your time and attention are relentless and more than you can possibly accomplish, it is very useful to impose some discipline and carefully evaluate which initiatives merit a spot at the top of your to-do list. That is a lot easier than it sounds and the time these techniques can save you by preventing you from taking on unworthy tasks is an impressive return on this investment. You will find that once you've used them for a while, they just become part of the way you think.

Big Rocks

My mentor, Dr. James Cash, professor and former chairman of the MBA program at Harvard Business School, shared a metaphor years ago that has stayed with me ever since. He talked about filling a jar with rocks until they brim over the top. He asked if the jar appeared full, but then pointed out that there was still space between the rocks to fit in pebbles. Again, he asked if the jar was full, but now mentioned how sand could still fill in the small spaces between the pebbles. Finally, he noted that water could fill in the micro-gaps between the grains of sand. His point became quite clear: you could fit quite a lot into a jar if you start with the big stuff first.

If you put the trivial matters, the metaphorical sand, in your jar (schedule) first and then try to layer on the big rocks, you'll find that you have less room for the more important matters. What sand are you allowing to keep you from getting to some of your big rocks? Make a point from now on to consciously focus on the things that matter most to you. Give them the priority they deserve when allocating your time, resources, and attention.

Importance/Urgency Matrix

One of the most powerful and commonly used prioritization tools is a very simple importance/urgency matrix. First, it can be used to triage your "inbox" and help you decide whether a given task is worth doing and how quickly it should be addressed. It looks like this:

	Urgent	*Not Urgent*
Important	Immediate Priority	Planning and Preparation/ Renewal Activities
Not Important	Interruptions	Busywork

If something is urgent and important, it zooms to the top of your to-do list. If something is not important and not time sensitive, it's likely to be busywork and doesn't merit your time. This item should populate your not-to-do-list.

The other two quadrants require judgment. If something is urgent, but not important, you need to decide if it is worth the effort. These are likely to be interruptions. Sometimes, it is almost as quick to address them as it is to dismiss them, and it can be worth the brief effort to satisfy someone else. Other times, what someone else is asking of you would take you away from something more pressing, so you're better off passing on it.

Important items that are not time sensitive require your attention. Often, these are activities like taking care of your health or doing some long-range planning—maybe even what you are doing right now. They often allow you to be more efficient and effective over the long term, but there's usually no burning need to address these items immediately. Because urgency isn't forcing you to address these matters, it's important to proactively make time on your calendar for them. If you don't make a point of finding the time, they will likely continue to be pushed to the back burner until they fall off the stove altogether. They may never get your attention, or worse, they will hang over your head as a nagging undone chore. Vacations and spiritual renewal activities fall into this category as well. Taking breaks to refresh and renew often does not feel urgent, but it is essential.

As a visually oriented thinker, I like to use this grid to look at how the many potential projects compare to one another as they compete for limited time. To show you how this looks, let's go back to Mark's list of activities. I've altered the grid slightly to show relative importance and urgency so that it now presents more of a continuum than absolute values.

MARK'S GOALS AND PRIORITIES

	More Urgent	*Less Urgent*
High Importance	Autism Run Exercise	Dinner Dates
Low Importance		Community Service Firm Events

Mark assigned exercise the highest level of importance and it was very urgent as well. And while finding a wife was at least as important to him, it didn't feel quite as urgent as getting his blood pressure under control. He found he was not terribly motivated to participate in community service activities sponsored by his law firm. Initially, he thought that would be an easy way to fulfill the obligation he felt to contribute to worthy causes. However, when he looked at that activity relative to the other things on his list, the programs his firm supported just didn't move him. That came off his list. Just before he came to our coaching session, his sister told him about a ten-kilometer road race to raise money for an agency that provides services and advocacy for children with autism. Because training for that race would contribute to both his fitness and community service goals, that rocketed to the highest importance quadrant. And because he had to be ready to run by the predetermined date just a few weeks away, this effort took on the highest urgency.

Mark also confessed that he hoped he'd meet some single, community-minded women at the race as well, making that a potential "three-fer." So he went right to work training for that race. He also committed to setting up some dinner dates. While not as urgent, reconnecting with friends and family was important to adding some joy back into his days. He was able to accomplish this by scheduling dinners with family and friends a little later in the evening without competing with his other priorities.

Will This Work? Feasibility Filters

Once you have prioritized your initiatives in terms of importance and time sensitivity, you'll want to look at which strategies are most likely to help you achieve a given goal. In business, we're trained to look at return on investment. This is usually expressed in financial terms. If you invest a hundred dollars in X, you'll make a thousand dollars profit. For your life plan, you will look at how to invest your time and attention to get the biggest payoff for the least effort, leaving as much time as possible to invest on other endeavors. Also, you'll need to address the fact that the more difficult something is to accomplish, the higher the risk that it might not work at all.

Risk/Reward Matrix

I've developed a tool I call the Risk/Reward Matrix to evaluate the difficulty of implementing certain strategies relative to their potential benefit. If something is easy to do and is going to pay huge dividends, pursuing it is a no brainer. Likewise, if something is difficult to achieve and won't yield much benefit, it's clear that you'd cross that off your list. Judgment again becomes a factor where something is easy to do but produces relatively little benefit. You'll also need to decide if it's worth investing in something that may be difficult to carry out, but comes with huge rewards if achieved.

		Reward/Payoff	
		High	**Low**
Risk/Difficulty/ Resource Requirement	**Low**	Must do	Quick hits—fine if you have the time
	High	The impact may be huge, but not guaranteed; evaluate the effort required against the likelihood of achievement	Add to *not-to-do* list

You can use this grid to evaluate each strategy you are contemplating on its own merits or in relation to other items on your list. To maximize your chances for success, strive to choose the actions that will give you the biggest payoff for your efforts and that will play to your strengths. Remember to balance the portfolio of strategies you select to reflect the mix of priorities you set for yourself.

This grid can also be used to evaluate the relative cost/benefit of the many strategies you're considering. Let's look at how Mark used it to guide his thinking about developing his exercise program. You will consider the risks and benefits on a continuum and create a picture of how the initiatives rate relative to one another.

MARK'S EXERCISE PROGRAM STRATEGIES

		Reward/Payoff	
		Higher	*Lower*
Risk/Difficulty/Resource Requirement	**Higher**	Hike the Himalayas Play tennis	Build home gym Join hiking club
	Lower	Join gym Running	

Mark's matrix led him to decide to start running before breakfast several days a week. It was not only great exercise, all he needed was a decent weather forecast and the discipline to put on his sneakers and go. To top it off, several of his friends were runners and he had a natural gift for organizing groups. He set up a system so they could notify each other when they were heading out; that way, group members could easily meet up for company and encouragement. That met his social and health goals. Joining a gym also rose to the top of his strategies list, since it allowed him to exercise in bad weather. While there was a cost to gym membership that running did not have, and Mark had to drive to the health club, the benefit of membership was well worth the expense because it rounded out his fitness routine. Tennis also made the list because he enjoyed it so much. However, when it came to adding tennis to his schedule, Mark viewed it as a complement to running and his gym routine, because court time was expensive and required more intricate scheduling to meet friends at the club.

He took things off his list, starting with building a home gym. The ease of rolling out of bed to work out in his PJs wasn't worth the expense of the equipment and it offered no social opportunity. He also crossed the Himalayan trekking expedition off his list. While it would be a very cool trip, the fitness benefits would be short lived and the logistics were extremely complicated. Last, Mark removed joining a hiking club from his list. His SWOT reflected that he is not a good "joiner." He likes being in charge rather than following someone else's itinerary. He also knew that finding the time for group outings would be difficult at best. Besides, his health club membership satisfied the physical and social benefits he would realize from joining a hiking club, and it therefore offered minimal incremental value.

Personal Power Grid

Organization consultants and psychologists Dennis Jaffe and Cynthia Scott created the final matrix I present here, called a Personal Power Grid.[1] This is another excellent filter to evaluate whether your efforts will have the impact you seek. It can also help you see how your own behavior either propels you toward fulfilling your vision, stalls your progress, or pulls you off course altogether.

	Can Control Outcome	*Cannot Control Outcome*
Take Action	Mastery	Ceaseless Striving
Take No Action	Giving Up	Letting Go

In this instance, mastery means taking action when you know it is going to pay off. If Mark exercises regularly and follows his nutritionist's advice, he will lose weight. That's mastery, and what you should be aiming for whenever possible. If Mark decides to throw up his hands and not make the effort to work out, that's giving up. Copping out is another term for knowing what you need to do and choosing not to do it.

Taking action when you can't control the outcome is what the authors of this grid call ceaseless striving. People pleasers take note: one of the most insidious time wasters falls in this category if you're continually trying to win the approval of someone whom you've not been able to please in the past, no matter how extreme your efforts. Many of us spin our wheels at some point. How many people are yo-yo dieters? Every time they start a new regimen, they are convinced that *this* time it will be different. Is that really true? There's a popular definition of insanity—doing the same thing over and over but expecting a different result. If you find yourself in this situation, take some time to figure out what's driving your behavior and what it is costing you—especially in relation to what else you could be doing to achieve your goal.

On the other hand, if you cannot control the outcome of a situation and you choose not to act, there's grace in letting go. This is another way to populate your not-to-do list. I can't play foosball to save my life. Do you think I'm being modest? A four-year-old once refused to have me on his team because I'm so lousy at it. No matter how much I practice, I just can't get good at flipping plastic footballers on a metal rod. While my ego may not like conceding a lack of talent in any area, spending any more time on that worthless pursuit would be wasted effort. Now I just play Ping-Pong with that kid. I can even beat him on that table, thank you very much.

Toolbox

Serenity Prayer

If you have a hard time letting go, try reciting this prayer that is a common fixture in the recovery movement:

Grant me the serenity to accept the things I cannot change; the courage to change the things I can; and the wisdom to know the difference.

But beware of giving up and calling it letting go. When my daughter moved up to high school, she was the only kid in her eighth grade class to be recommended for Advanced Placement Math, the highest level available. My daughter's teacher cautioned her that she'd be mixed in with the best math students in town and that she'd have to work hard to earn a "C" grade. She agreed, and took on the challenge. Sure enough, it was a real struggle. Her new teacher sent her several notes suggesting she see him for extra help. Accustomed to breezing through her lessons unaided, she opted to keep trying on her own—until she'd had enough and told me she wanted to drop down into Honors Math. Fortunately, her teacher had told me that one of the goals of AP Math was teaching students how to learn when learning is hard. That's something these kids had not yet experienced.

I told my daughter that if she gave AP Math everything she had and it was still too hard for her, it would be just fine for her to drop to a level where she might learn more. However, I knew she could still accept the extra help her teacher offered and there may have been other available avenues for help that she hadn't pursued. I explained that she was learning to use new intellectual muscles, and like lifting weights for the first time, the effort can leave you feeling sore. But with perseverance, the pain goes away and eventually you can lift more and more weight. So she hung in there, got the help she needed, and did just fine. That effort moved her into the mastery quadrant on the personal power grid. Had she given up without making that extra effort, she never would have discovered the true limits of her abilities. However, if she made the effort and the math was still too hard, she could have let go of the notion she belonged in AP Math and gracefully moved into a class that was a better match for her abilities.

It is worth the effort to be sure you're not giving up too soon or hanging on too long. That's not always clear before you've given something a try. So, you can also use this grid after you've implemented a strategy to help you evaluate whether it's worth continuing or whether you'd be better off trying something new.

Joy Meter

Remember that your emotions give you important information about how well something is aligned with your values and your purpose. This is actually a very practical statement. You are much more likely to stick with something you enjoy doing. I always find visual reminders helpful for decision making, particularly because our heads often have a tendency to overrule our hearts. That's why I created the joy meter and presented it in a toolbox for goal setting. And because we're trying to maximize joy along with optimizing outcomes, we need to keep our joy quotient front and center in our calculus of which activities merit our attention.

Diane, the physician who was looking to raise her professional profile, kept a clear focus on her joy quotient at work. She had so thoroughly researched the issues related to prescribing narcotics in order to write a policy manual that her knowledge on the subject was on a par with any leading authority. And she so thoroughly enjoyed being a subject matter expert that she had set a goal to contribute to the national discourse on this important topic. So she came to her coaching session to explore strategies to create a platform to share her expertise on a broader stage. She also had to address the practical necessity of finding funding to support this endeavor if it meant giving up clinical time to do it.

We reviewed the options open to her. The traditional course in her discipline would be to present at national and international conferences. However, that would require a great deal of travel and would be in direct conflict with her goal of being home as much as possible for her young family. I asked her if she'd considered blogging on the topic and establishing herself as an online thought leader. This was so far out of the norm in medicine that it hadn't even ocurred to her. But it appealed in many ways. First, she loved writing and could do it from home. Second, she'd be blazing new trails and it looked like a niche she could claim for her own.

We then turned our attention to how she would replace the salary she would lose by giving up a clinical session to free up time for this new endeavor. It was clear that the traditional funding sources were unlikely to pay her to blog. But she had come across a few resources during her research that she thought might support her if she turned some of her posts into white papers that could be used by other health-care leaders. We also discussed some foundations that might give her a grant for this worthy endeavor. Finally, she agreed to check into the feasibility of setting up a proprietary website and charging a subscription fee to access her policy suggestions. Alternatively, we discussed her posting the information free of charge, but charging for phone consultations to help hospitals and clinics with writing their own policy manuals. The consulting idea especially appealed to her as it would add significantly to her joy quotient, pushing that strategy up high in her rankings.

EXERCISE

Rank and Select Your Strategies

Grab your notebook and closet. Review your checklist, goals, and priorities. Start with the immediate-term items and record your plan for addressing each one. For those without an obvious approach, brainstorm all of the possible strategies you can think of to accomplish your goals. It's often useful to ask a close friend, family member, or mentor to help you with this exercise. Use the tools presented in this chapter to rank your immediate-term items according to their ease of accomplishment and likelihood to produce the desired result. Select the top candidates. (Make sure to keep the whole list so you can revisit your options if the selected approach proves less effective than predicted.) Then look at your medium- and long-range goals and make sure you have strategies in place to address those at the appropriate times. Rank your strategies and record them in your notebook.

Once you've selected your top strategies, put them on a shelf in your closet. Create a recurring appointment on your calendar to check your closet at regular intervals to monitor your progress and revise your approach as needed. Remember to take a moment to celebrate your successes, no matter how small. There's great joy in making progress, so be sure to soak it all in and give yourself the credit you deserve.

Make Every Day Count

All of these tools can be adapted for everyday use. Each morning, I set aside time to set an intention for the day. I think about what I want to accomplish, how I want to feel, and anything else of importance. I use this time to zero in on my two or three "big rocks" and commit to accomplishing them before allowing any sand to distract me. This is a good time to think about your priorities in a balanced way—whatever balance means for you.

Step ❽ Get Going

Your Simplementation Plan™

"A journey of a thousand miles begins with a single step."[1]

—Lao-Tzu

The time to act has arrived. If you're the "let's just get in the car and start driving" type, this comes as welcome news. For others, it's not easy to embark on a new adventure, no matter how exciting the destination. You've completed all the preliminaries, so grab your compass, map, and walking stick (or your vision, goals, and strategies) and set out on the path toward fulfilling your dreams. There's no time like the present.

Start Simply, but Simply Start

How will you begin executing the strategies for achieving your most pressing priorities? At this point in the Business of Life workshops, I have people pair up and talk to their partners about what they will do in the next *day* to move forward, start a new venture, work on restoring balance, or simply grace their days with more joy notes. With a room full of witnesses, they commit to making it happen. Now it is your turn.

I know. The idea of starting to "live the life of my dreams" may be so daunting that it paralyzes you and nestles you even more firmly into the well-worn rut you've occupied for some time. So how do you suddenly burst into action? By starting small and creating what I call your "simplementation plan."

Neuroscientists know that the human brain is wired to resist change. It's a dilemma that stops a lot of people dead in their tracks. Contemplating any shift that requires a significant departure from your normal routine can be frightening. Your brain senses your fear and triggers the "fight or flight" reaction that floods your body with chemicals to prepare you to cope with dangerous situations. Because your brain can't always distinguish between the types of threats you face, this primitive response can actually send you running away from the idea of initiating a job search just as fast as if you were being chased down by a saber-toothed tiger. Early in our evolution, such an extreme response made sense. But now that most of us don't have to worry about being someone's lunch, it can be a bit much. In order to deal with the immediate and potentially fatal threat of a snarling predator, your brain actually shuts down other functions so you can channel all of your energy into running for cover. When the "threat" is emotional stress, it can shut down your ability to tackle the very issue you need to focus on most.

So what's the answer? Persuade your brain that the change is something it can handle. The trick is to keep taking small steps and let all those little things add up to something big. By asking your brain to accept small, incremental changes, you bypass the fight-or-flight response. That's the premise behind kaizen, the Japanese term for "change for the better." It's about taking small steps to achieve a goal and pursue continuous improvement.[2]

The great news is that your brain is plastic, meaning that it reshapes itself throughout your life. As you learn new skills or acquire new habits, connections between brain cells called neurons are established or strengthened. If you do take those small steps and keep at it, those connections become stronger until the new routines become second nature. Alternatively, your brain prunes away connections that aren't used over time.[3] This is a use-it-or-lose-it system. The key is to get started and persevere until your brain adapts to help you make the new habit stick.

Break It Down

You don't eat a watermelon by trying to sink your teeth into the uncut whole. You can't get your mouth around the rind and it isn't particularly tasty either. But if you cut it open, there are soft, sweet chunks that are easy—and delicious—to eat. You will take one small step at a time until you build up some momentum and become an unstoppable force moving toward your vision. Nothing begets success like success. So to get you started and keep you motivated, this chapter will focus on how to keep your vision quest simple while you master the art of breaking a big journey down into walkable steps.

You Are Just a First Step Away

Peggy and Gail, the artists who wanted to start an art therapy program for kids with cancer, were overwhelmed with the idea of launching a nonprofit organization, creating a business plan, establishing a fundraising program, and on and on. In fact, when we finished mapping out the steps they'd have to go through to carry out their plan, they were pretty much convinced they'd bitten off more than they could chew. My job, however, is to leave my clients feeling empowered to act, so we couldn't finish our session until that was accomplished. I looked for ways to work with their natural wiring so they could find something in their wheelhouse that they could accomplish that would give them a sense of progress and possibility. Because they are both visual artists, the assignment I designed appealed to that sensibility. I sent them to a nearby art supply store to buy the most beautiful file folders they could find. The next day, they gathered all their loose papers and organized them into those pretty folders. They popped them into a file cabinet and, voilà! Our Space, Inc. had an office. It can be that simple to begin.

Creating a base of operations for Our Space was clearly an important and urgent goal. Choosing attractive folders—the very act of taking such a concrete step—registered a decidedly positive "joy-to-hassle ratio" on their joy meter. On the Risk/Reward Matrix, buying office supplies was a very low-risk effort and the reward was also relatively small when viewed against the goal of launching a whole organization. But it had an enormous payoff in that doing something so tangible had the critical effect of moving Peggy and Gail from being dreamers to doers. That simple act changed their whole perception of their ability to achieve their vision because it set them on a path where each step led to the next small, doable task.

Setting up the file system also convinced them that they could organize themselves even further. They pulled out their SWOT and decided to focus on their strengths first. They needed to build a base of support for Our Space, Inc. both for program development and for fundraising. They noted that they had an inspiring mission and vision and, as cancer survivors themselves, had a compelling message. They decided the next logical step was to develop some printed materials that would help them communicate their mission to people who could help them get the effort up and running. They also had some aptitude for writing, so this played to their strengths. Next, they used their artistic skills to design a logo, create some stationery, and print some business cards. Day by day, Our Space was closer to becoming a reality. Each successful step energized Gail and Peggy and led them to the next logical task.

Just Do It

The journey toward a new career can begin with a single phone call, followed by a commitment to make another one every day, asking for an informational interview. Just do something on your list related to your dream, no matter how trivial it seems. Accomplishing the first small thing is incentive to take the next step, then the next. And soon it's a quick jog toward your destination.

EXERCISE

Take Action—Create Your Simplementation Plan

Go through your rank-ordered list of strategies and choose one or more that you can initiate *today* that will set you on your way to achieving one of your goals. What concrete action will you take to get started? What is the next task you will undertake to keep moving forward? Commit to taking at least one small action each day until you achieve that goal. Because you are far more likely to do something if you plan a specific time and place to tackle it, make an appointment on your calendar each day to attend to whatever task you've selected. Then honor that commitment as you would any other appointment. You are worth it.

When Simplementing Doesn't Seem So Simple

Most of us can find the equivalent of Peggy and Gail's file folders—that one small step we can take to get started implementing our strategies. But what do you do if a good first step for each part of your action plan isn't so clear or if you face other obstacles that make it hard to get started? The following sections address some of the common challenges that can stand in the way of progress. We will look at some examples of how people got over (or around) their blocks and on their way. However, please note that the recommendations presented here are not a substitute for clinical care. If you are experiencing serious distress, please consider seeing a trained professional to help identify the root of your difficulties and prescribe the appropriate treatment.

> *"Almost all quality improvement comes via simplification of design, manufacturing...layout, processes, and procedures."*[4]
>
> —Tom Peters

As you've no doubt noticed by now, keeping your tasks simple and doable is one of the greatest keys to successful implementation of your well-crafted plans. If you've completed all the steps in the planning process, you have carefully considered what you want to do and how you want to do it. People tend to make matters much more complicated than they need to be. That tendency makes it hard to do things and even harder to do them well. So let's take a look at how you can cut through the complexity and get going when the going seems tough.

Implementing When Inertia Overwhelms Your Resolve

Change is hard, even when it's good. And it's especially hard when your current pattern is as well worn and cozy as your favorite pair of furry slippers. When you're stuck in a rut, any shift can seem so overwhelming that finding the energy to make such a major move seems truly impossible.

My coaching clients frequently find it helpful to get geared up to take that first step by reviewing what it's costing them to stay put. Reminding yourself what motivated you to start this process in the first place is often enough to nudge you in a new direction.

Danielle got her wake-up call that day in her Business of Life workshop when she discovered that she had not employed most of her creative talents nor pursued any of her passions in her twenty-year career as a fashion buyer. But staying in an industry where she was so well established was her path of least resistance. She'd been so comfortably uncomfortable there for so long, it was daunting to even contemplate doing anything else. That day in her workshop, she confronted for the first time what staying put would cost her. It would continue to rob her of experiencing the joy she knew she could find doing something else.

What that something else was wasn't entirely clear just yet, but one fact was evident. As long as she stayed where she was, nothing was going to change. Her first step was to leave her current company even as they offered her a promotion and ever-bigger bonuses. Simple enough. Easy? Not at all. Danielle needed to acknowledge that disentangling herself from her current situation was indeed taking action toward her new future. It was a critically important first step. Doing so would actually create the space she needed to consider her next steps.

Sure enough, contemplating so much free time was truly frightening to this high-powered executive who was so used to getting up at dawn to exercise before her marathon days at work. But she'd finally had enough and was ready to accept that the risk of not finding and pursuing her passion was greater than taking the leap.

After finally leaving her job, Danielle gave herself a few weeks to clean out her closets and play with her puppy. She took some time to take long walks on the beach near her house that she'd not been around to fully enjoy. Those walks gave her time and space to think about what she wanted to do next. She also had a shocking revelation: from the day she left her office, she'd not missed being there for a single moment. That realization made her feel like she was finally free to contemplate the future without looking back.

Danielle wasn't ready to make big decisions about her next job, but she was ready for a little fun. She went back to her closet and zeroed in on her short-term goal of taking a cooking class. Her husband had recently given her a gift certificate for just such a class, so she signed up right away. Stepping into the school's kitchen felt so great to Danielle that she had a strong feeling that she was exactly where she was meant to be. She felt so happy there, like she was finally in her element. This newfound joy was something she could get used to.

Implementing When the Task Seems Too Big

When the prospect of starting a new project seems too daunting because of its sheer size or just its newness, it's natural to feel overwhelmed and let your nervous neurons get the better of you. This is especially true for the chronic procrastinator. If this rings a bell with you, a simplementation plan may be just what you need to get going. Martin was a corporate vice president who procrastinated by heeding the call to solve his colleague's crisis du jour to the detriment of his own projects. He actually got a little rush of adrenaline every time he helped put out a fire and he enjoyed the sense of accomplishment. He finally conquered his penchant for putting off his own projects by igniting a little drama for himself.

Martin needed to present a report on the state of his industry to his company's board of directors in three months' time and had put off starting this enormous undertaking for several weeks already. The looming deadline made him nervous enough that he enlisted the help of one of his fellow vice presidents and asked her to hold him accountable for turning in the various analyses he needed to complete his white paper.

To raise the stakes, she invited him to share his findings at her weekly department head meetings. He ended each presentation with a promise of what he would discuss at the following meeting. By giving himself a deadline and a roomful of colleagues whose own work depended on his completing these tasks, he suddenly had a burning platform. While the idea of writing the magnum opus on the entire industry overwhelmed him and drove him to keep putting it off, each individual analysis was something he could wrap his brain around and accomplish. Having an audience for the individual components appealed to his desire to feel appreciated and created the sense of urgency that he needed to swing into action mode. It took advantage of his wiring and it worked like a charm. Martin finished his report with two weeks to spare.

Implementing When Fear Stands in the Way

Brenda's math phobia had kept her from pursuing the college degree that was necessary for fulfilling her dream to have a career in management. A root cause analysis helped her identify the source of that problem—the middle school teacher who humiliated her in front of her classmates and told her she had no talent for math. It didn't even take five whys to get to the core of her problem.

Why have I been unable to obtain a management position?
I don't have the college degree most require.

Why don't I have a college degree?
I'm afraid I can't pass the math courses.

Why am I afraid of failing math?
My middle school teacher told me I have no aptitude for math.

Now that we knew the root of her problem, we could address it. In our coaching sessions, Brenda acknowledged that, in fact, she used mathematics every day in her job and that her teacher was simply wrong. But letting go of that long-held belief wasn't as simple as it sounds. She had so fully identified with the label of math failure that accepting that the opposite was true required a leap of faith that was hard to take.

She was filled with dread as she prepared to register for her first college math course at age forty. Taking that initial step was so hard for her that we had to review her options. If she didn't conquer her fear, it was highly unlikely she'd ever have the management career she so dearly desired. The opportunity cost of not taking that first step was high indeed. When asked what's the worst that could happen if she did take the course, she said she might flunk out. She had to admit, however, that while it would be another blow to her self-esteem, she'd be no worse off than she already was. And if she conquered her fear, she just might have a shot at her dream. That was enough to drive her into action. She registered for her first class that very day.

If fear is holding you back, try asking yourself the same questions Brenda considered. Then determine for yourself what is more frightening—never reaching your full potential or facing down a worry that's been limiting your prospects all along.

Implementing When Your Plan Isn't Perfect Yet

Perfectionists often have trouble starting and finishing projects. Starting because the plan isn't watertight. Finishing because it's never 100 percent "right." Well, I've got news for you. No matter how "right" you get your plan, you are most likely going to have to work with other people to make it all happen. People are messy creatures who seem to like doing things their own way. Try as you might, you will never be able to control everything and everyone. So you need to prepare as well as you can and then find the courage to let go.

If it helps, remind yourself you don't have to be perfect to be helpful. In fact, showing your vulnerability just might be a gift that you can give to others. I once gave a talk at a high-stakes conference and was mortified when I couldn't recall a word and stumbled through a short section of my speech. I was beside myself that these leaders of industry caught me in a moment of imperfection. So imagine my surprise—and delight—when the line of people coming up to talk to me at the end of the program snaked all the way out of the ballroom. One after another, the attendees thanked me for inspiring them and making the material so "relatable." Those mumbling moments ended up being an important ingredient in the cement that created such a powerful bond with the audience. I won't go so far as to recommend tripping over your words just to seem "real," but do just take a deep breath and know that often "really good" is as close to perfect as you need to be.

Implementing When There Are Not Enough Hours in the Day

"I don't have enough time to…" is the common refrain of people with the yeah-but habit. There are so many things you'd like to be doing, *but* you just don't have the time. *But*, there are too many other things competing for your attention. The *but*s never end. The fact is you have the same twenty-four hours a day that everyone else has. How you spend that time is an expression of your priorities. Without a doubt, there are many things you must do. But it's unlikely that you can't free up *any* time to accommodate a new priority. If that *is* the case, the new thing isn't truly your highest priority.

If you find yourself in this position and you didn't free up enough space on your schedule in the time and emotion exercise, there's one more thing you can try.

You can perform something called a paired comparison test to assess whether everything that is currently on your calendar is more important and urgent than the new task you are having trouble accommodating.

To accomplish this, take out your notebook and your calendar. For each item on your schedule, assign an importance score from one (least important) to five (most important). Then do the same for each of the activities you'd like to accommodate that don't currently fit. Create a grid like the one below and record the relative scores. The first number in each box is the importance of the item on the left side of the grid. The second number corresponds to the item along the top. This grid allows you to look at the relative importance of each entry in comparison with everything else on your schedule.

PAIRED COMPARISON TEST

	Exercise	Work	Family Dinners	Watch TV	Read Novels	Read Trade Journals	Sleep
Exercise	5/5	5/5	5/5	5/2	5/4	5/5	5/5
Work	5/5	5/5	5/5	5/2	5/4	5/5	5/5
Family Dinners	5/5	5/5	5/5	5/2	5/4	5/5	5/5
Watch TV	2/5	2/5	2/5	2/2	5/4	2/5	2/5
Read Novels	4/5	4/5	4/5	4/2	4/4	4/5	4/5
Read Trade Journals	5/5	5/5	5/5	5/2	5/4	5/5	5/5
Sleep	5/5	5/5	5/5	5/2	5/4	5/5	5/5

In this example, the new activity I want to add is reading trade journals. I believe this will add to my knowledge base and prepare me to achieve my goal of getting a promotion at work. It's a top priority. When I look at everything else currently on my schedule, there's not much there that isn't a high priority. The only two things that don't rank a five are my downtime activities of reading novels (which rates a four) and watching television (which rates a two). I need a little breathing time, so I'm not willing to give up both. But I see when I look at it this way that I generally prefer reading novels to watching TV. Because reading trade journals rates a five, I need to make time for that. So, reluctantly, I decide to give up television. Then I challenge my own all-or-nothing thinking and realize I don't have to go cold turkey. If I read trade journals three days a week, I can probably keep up on the latest industry trends. That allows me to watch my favorite programs the other four days a week. Whew.

Try this exercise for yourself. If everything rates a tie, that tells you something already. Is everything you're doing *really* as important as you think? If yes, go ahead and rank each item with an urgency score and repeat the comparison. What can wait and be done once you've accomplished something that is more time sensitive?

Take a critical look at your chart. Make some decisions; then make a switch. Or make peace with your assessment if you decide you're already doing everything that is most urgent and important.

Just Get Moving

If creating your simplementation plan was simple for you, you're ready to act. If it was less so, use all the tools in your kit and make your plan now. Then look at what you've committed to doing within the next day and do it. You are only a small first step away from making your dreams come true.

I know how frightening this can be. If I'd given in to my own fears, I wouldn't have sung in public after my third-grade music teacher silenced me for decades. But I faced my deepest insecurity and here I am, stronger than ever, to tell the tale.

Whatever is holding you back, consider carefully whether you're better off staying put or forging ahead. If you choose moving forward, realize that it's unlikely to get easier, so you might as well hold your nose and jump. And once you've done it, you can jump for joy.

How Is It Going?

The hardest part is over. You've set out on your path and are on your way toward fulfilling your vision. If all is going well, you have added the grace notes that make each day a pleasure and fill your reservoirs of joy. You're making steady progress and enjoying the journey.

But how do you know if it's going well or not? Remember the importance of cultivating presence and awareness. Pay attention to how you feel and whether or not you are advancing toward the accomplishment of your goals. In keeping with your newly formed habits, you will not leave this to chance. You will schedule appointments on your calendar to check in at regular intervals to see how you're doing.

EXERCISE

Evaluate Your Progress

Where are you relative to where you want to be? Now that you've taken some strategic steps forward, have you:

- Maintained a focus on your priorities?
- Used your gifts and talents?
- Achieved some goals?
- Made progress toward others?
- Kept joy in the picture?

Are your strategies working well?

- Yes? Keep going.
- No? Make some adjustments to your current approach or try something else on your list of potential strategies. Reviewing

the Personal Power Grid in step 7 may be useful to help you be sure you're not giving up too soon. But if, after giving your strategy your best shot, it's still not working, there is grace in letting go. As W.C. Fields once said, "If at first you don't succeed, try, try again. Then quit. No use being a damn fool about it."[5]

Are you enjoying the process?
Are your strategies fueling you or leaving you feeling drained?

- Fueling? Keep going.
- Draining? Is there a more pleasant way to approach the goal?

Do you have SMART (specific, measurable, attainable, realistic, timely) goals? If so, determine the appropriate metrics to evaluate those particular goals. Be specific about measuring your progress. For example, the metrics for your exercise program could be the number of times you made it to the gym each week over the past month. You may have a fitness measure you'd like to track such as the duration and intensity of your workouts over time and your endurance levels. If your exercise is meant to contribute to a weight loss goal, you might want to get on the scale weekly and track that as well.

Toolbox

Gut Check

Your emotions provide you with important information about how well your actions are aligned with your sense of joy and purpose. As you review your progress, how do you *feel* about the way it's going? Respect what your feelings are telling you.

Set Your Check-In Schedule

How often should you track your progress? The appropriate interval is determined by what you are trying to accomplish. Depending on what is on your list, you may want to track your initiatives separately. If one goal is to get in shape by exercising regularly, weekly reviews of your success in getting to the gym might be fitting. If you are working on the cure for cancer, you'll have to give yourself a much longer time frame. While you'll want to track your progress toward that overall goal, you are likely to have broken it down into several initiatives. Perhaps you are a scientist and you set goals of:

- Getting a job at an academic medical center
- Establishing a research laboratory
- Hiring a staff
- Securing funding

You will need to evaluate each of these goals on its own as well as in relation to one another. You'll need the appointment at the medical school before you can establish a laboratory. You may get start-up funding when you land your job, but then you'll have to demonstrate some results in order to get federal grants to continue your research.

Whatever your goals, give careful consideration to the appropriate time frame to measure your success. Choose a window that will give your strategy a sufficient opportunity to prove its worth, but not so much that you lose precious time if it isn't effective. Be sure to do a careful assessment so you don't continue to pursue activities that prevent your forward motion.

Once again, put a recurring appointment on your calendar to review your closet to ensure you are making good progress toward your goals. Many Business of Life graduates tell me that years after taking their class, they're still looking in their closets to stay focused on their priorities. They make adjustments as necessary and enjoy seeing their successes. It simply works.

Enjoy the Ride

You are on your way. If you've completed all eight steps, you are well prepared to move toward the vision that sets you aglow. Stay present and alert to what you're doing so you will continually make conscious choices about how you spend your precious time.

You can repeat any of the assessment and alignment exercises in this book periodically to make sure you stay the course or alter your approach if your evolving circumstances call for a change in direction. You will want to stick with your plans as long as they serve you, but you don't want to be so rigid that you become stuck in a new rut. Be open to new possibilities. You now have a powerful framework for evaluating how well they fit into your plans.

As you saw with Martin's experience, being accountable to someone else is a great way to ensure you make regular progress. Knowing that you will have to tell someone else what you've accomplished greatly increases the odds that you will have something significant to report. At the end of my Business of Life programs, everyone is assigned a buddy and I encourage them to schedule regular dates to check in with one another. I recommend you do the same. Find a friend or colleague who is interested in your undertaking. Schedule regular check-ins, whether by e-mail, phone, or in person, and take a few moments to update your "buddy" on your progress. Beyond giving you an incentive to keep moving, this serves as an opportunity to discuss any challenges you may be facing and brainstorm potential solutions.

One last thing: remember to celebrate your triumphs. Share your success stories. Honor your efforts and inspire someone else. That will add to your joy quotient—which in turn will fuel you to keep on keeping on.

Step Back: Tips and Tools to Get Back on Track and Stay the Course

"No matter how far you have gone on a wrong road, turn back."
—Turkish proverb

Strategic planning is a neat, methodical, and dependable process that, in a perfect world, would give us neat, methodical, and dependable results. Though wondrous, the world is far from perfect and life can be messy. History, habits, and happenstance can conspire to pull our best-laid plans off course. Did you run into difficulty as you set your priorities and made your plans? What's been getting in your way? I have yet to encounter anyone who doesn't have something that causes them to make suboptimal choices from time to time. Often it's something as straightforward as watching too much television or constantly succumbing to digital distractions. For others, more ingrained behaviors pull them off course.

Strategies to Get Back on Track

Becoming aware of what is pulling you off track from making steady progress is a great first step toward recalibrating the way you make decisions going forward. The techniques presented in this section may also be helpful if you found yourself back in step 4 identifying with one or more of the descriptions of people with an inclination toward:

- People pleasing
- Perfectionism
- Inertia
- Ego identification and control issues
- Listening to naysayers
- Succumbing to the yeah-but habit
- Procrastination

Cultivate Conscious Awareness

As obvious as this may sound, it's important to pay attention to the reasons you make decisions that create situations you consider less than optimal. What compels you to cede your power to someone else or just react to whatever comes your way rather than steering your own ship? If you are prone to inertia, staying the course even when it no longer suits you, be alert to any nagging sensations of vague dissatisfaction. It may behoove you to perform regular gut checks to see how you're feeling about your current lot. Use the joy meter to keep tabs.

Remember that you will never get "there." As soon as you bag one peak, you'll be off looking for the next hill to conquer. That is part of the human condition, especially for high achievers. Just remember to enjoy the climb. Be aware of what is enough for *you*. Avoid mindlessly going after more just for the sake of more.

Strive for Acceptance;
Set Reasonable Expectations

Many of us spin our wheels because we think we can or should change the essential nature of things. This is a common pitfall for people who have control issues. They want things the way they want them, even when that's an unreasonable expectation. I'm always bemused by people who buy hunting dogs and then get angry with them for behaving like hunters. Retrievers roll in smelly things when given a chance. That's what they do. It's unreasonable for humans to put this kind of canine in a house and then be upset with them for doing what is part of their essential nature, even though that behavior is not compatible with pristine housekeeping.

Likewise, a young mother was talking to me at work one day about how frustrated she was when her eight-year-old son put holes in the knees of an expensive suit she bought for him the first time he wore it. I asked her what she was thinking when she bought an eight-year-old boy fancy pants knowing full well he was tough on his clothing. She blushed with recognition at her mistake and vowed to buy him clothing one step up from disposable next time they had a formal event to attend. It's much easier to accept that some kids crawl on floors than to curse the holey knees.

You Are the Expert on You

There is no shortage of experts touting their point of view and exhorting you to embrace their wisdom. And you can learn a lot from them. However, no one knows you as well as you know yourself, so you need to be a critical consumer of advice and make decisions that make the most sense for you given your current circumstances.

This point was brought home to me when I had a stubborn hamstring injury that took years to heal. I'd been practicing yoga for years, all the while listening to several instructors touting the virtues of a vegetarian diet. Then my doctor referred me for acupuncture to try to improve the circulation near my injury to speed up healing. On my first visit, the acupuncturist did an assessment and declared that I didn't have enough meat in my diet. Both were giving sound dietary advice backed up with long history and good evidence for their perspective. And it's even possible that both are right—for some people at some time. My goal is to be healthy. How I achieve that health is up to me. Only I can decide what works best for me at any given time. Maybe more meat will be important when I get older and need more iron. I'll put that idea on a shelf in my closet and refer back to it in a few years if I feel the need for a change in my diet.

Humor Can Help

Armed with your mission and vision, you have some great tools to serve as filters that will help you define *your* priorities and what is most important to you. With these in your arsenal (and a sense of humor doesn't hurt either), you can stand firm in the face of others' suggestions and judgments. Not that I hold a grudge or anything, but about eighteen years ago, I met with a new colleague, an older and much more senior executive. He was of the strong opinion that women with young children (I had a two-year-old at the time) should stay at home to take care of them. He told me that his wife was a homemaker and you could "eat off his floors." I replied that you could eat off my floors too—and on a good day, you could find a whole meal. We moved on to the next topic.

It would have been easy to be intimidated by this man who outranked me, was significantly older, and was at least twice my size. However, I knew that my life's mission included a career and I had a clear set of priorities that achieved a balance of career, family, mind/body/spirit, and community activities that worked for me. Having examined my own priorities for myself before this conversation took place allowed me to laugh at the absurdity of what he was suggesting. Had I not known so clearly who I was as a well-rounded person who plays several different roles, I may have been vulnerable to his criticisms and likely to pack for the guilt trip he was trying to send me on. Instead, I bought a busy rug that hid the Cheerios.

Toolbox

Humor

Consider a witty retort when someone gives you unsolicited advice about what he thinks is right for you. With your mission and vision well articulated, *you* are the expert. Find a firm but lighthearted way to hold your ground.

Don't Let Yourself Be Shouldwinked

Who among us hasn't done something out of a sense of obligation, misplaced or not? We often say yes to something when we'd rather say no because we feel we should. This is especially common among pleasers and perfectionists, and it can be a real problem. My friend calls it "shoulding all over yourself." When you put it that way, it sounds especially unappealing.

I've been plenty guilty of this myself. One morning, my then ten-year-old daughter saw me eating my usual luscious breakfast of fat-free cottage cheese and bran nuggets. She asked me why I ate that and I told her that it was good for me. She asked if I liked it and I had to admit, not so much. That simple question was enough to bust me out of my inertia. That was the last day I ate "cottage cheese and crunchies" for breakfast just because I thought I should be eating something healthy. Lo and behold, there are tastier options. It was a great reminder that there's no dishonor in enjoying the journey.

Toolbox

Shed the Shoulds

What are your "cottage cheese and crunchies"—those things you do only because you feel you should? Is that really necessary? What would happen if you didn't do it or looked for a more pleasant way to accomplish the same objective?

Sharon, the vice president of a prestigious financial operation, signed up for my Business of Life course. A highly disciplined professional, she held such a stringent work ethic that she always felt she should eat her metaphorical vegetables before she could have dessert. During the session when people were recording their priorities, she was visibly upset. A couple of weeks later, as we were working on action plans, she broke down in tears. She had set spending more time with her daughter as a priority. Even as she did so, she felt the tug of the notion that always gnawed at her—that she *should* be attending to work matters instead of indulging in play with her child. The memory of a recent exchange with her six-year-old was what had her in tears. Sharon had promised to play a game one evening and asked if she could just make a quick business call before they started. Her daughter said no. Her business calls were never quick. Kids have a way of humbling us with the truth.

She came for a private coaching session to develop some strategies that would allow her to spend some guilt-free time with her child. Appealing to her strong sense of obligation, I asked her whose responsibility it was to nurture her child and model healthy behavior. She blanched at the realization that she was teaching her child to be a one-dimensional workaholic and admitted it was her job to spend quality time with her daughter. I recommended that she make playing with her kid a task that went right on her to-do list, alongside financial analyses and the laundry. If it made her feel any better, I conceded it could be an educational game, as long as she gave her child her undivided attention while they played. She needed to start thinking of time with her child as eating her spinach and not a chocolate éclair. That time was truly nourishing her child and their relationship. Showing Sharon that playing with her daughter was an item that merited a coveted spot on her to-do list worked with her wiring and helped her accept that it was at least as important and urgent as any business matter that threatened to invade her family time.

Step Back Before You React

Before saying yes to something you'd really rather not do, take a moment to assess what's really happening, what you're feeling and why you're feeling it. A good strategy for dealing with an unwelcome request is to say you'll need to think about it and get back to the person asking. Here are some good questions to ask when you see yourself slipping into some fear-driven behaviors:

- Why am I even considering this request/demand/expectation? Alternatively, why am I even considering *not* doing something about which I am passionately interested?
- What am I afraid of?
- Is my fear based on something real? If it is, so what?
- What if I don't do what someone's asking of me (or do what I want that someone else disapproves of)?
- What will it cost me to comply with their wishes?
- What's the worst thing that can happen? How bad is it really? What strategies can I employ to make the worst case not so bad?

Consider the Opportunity Cost

If you choose to do one thing, it likely means not being able to do another. What comes off the list to accommodate what you are contemplating taking on? Is it worthy or is it less important than the new activity? It's popular to advise a people pleaser to "learn to say no." Try flipping that around and discover what you want to say yes to. Then make conscious decisions that are in line with your own priorities.

It can also be helpful to remember that while those conversations in which you are saying no to someone's request can be uncomfortable, the discomfort dissipates shortly afterward. The tools and techniques in this book can help those talks go more smoothly. Remember that the discomfort of being "stuck" with a task that you've taken on reluctantly can cause you much more discomfort in the long run than the brief act of declining.

Toolbox

NO

There may be more power in the word "no" than any other two letters in the alphabet. I often assign my clients the task of saying no to five requests just to flex those muscles and see what happens. Often, people are surprised by how little resistance they actually meet. The filters in this chapter provide you with a vocabulary to explain your choices in a rational, objective, unemotional way that often helps your assertion to be accepted.

Use Compassion as a Tool

It's hard to feel intimidated by someone while you are feeling genuine compassion for her. As you can imagine, in my years as a senior executive in a large organization, I engaged in some pretty tense conversations, often when the stakes were very high. I happen to be petite and soft spoken and I like to think of myself as a kind person. But I couldn't be effective in my position if I were a pushover, so some confrontations were inevitable.

As a student of meditation techniques, I learned about compassion meditation, in which the practitioner focuses on a sincere desire for all suffering to cease. So I reasoned that if someone was acting in an aggressive manner, he must be suffering in some way. When I approached the encounter seeking to find out what was at the root of the negativity and to address it in a productive manner, I found I could confront the issue and the behavior without needing to attack the person in any way. In fact, the would-be confrontations often turned into cathartic conversations that cleared the way for productive problem solving. In some cases, we even emerged from these meetings with a stronger appreciation for one another.

Toolbox

Compassion

When you are facing a conversation where you fear the other person will respond in an angry or aggressive manner, try to be aware that pain of some sort is likely driving his behavior. Seek to address the cause of this discomfort and see if you can find a solution that satisfies the needs of the other person without sacrificing your own. Or, at the very least, to stand your ground without being intimidated.

The Tool Kit in Action

Let's take a look at how you might use a collection of these tools to change the outcome of a situation where you might be inclined to bend to another's wishes at the expense of your own priorities or desires.

Reframing a Bake Sale

I'd like to say no to making my hundredth batch of Rice Krispies Treats for the PTO, but there's Patsy, the cookie queen, looking like she's depending on me again. I always say yes to her, but this time, I *really* don't have time. Taking on the task this time is a threat to the work/life/health balance that's so important to my vision. What do I do? Asking the questions mentioned above can help evaluate and reframe the situation.

Why am I even considering this request? I'm afraid Patsy will be angry. Maybe she'll hate me and tell all the other mothers at the school that I'm a selfish so-and-so and they should have nothing to do with me. That'll hurt my feelings and I'm very sensitive.

Is it really true that she'll be angry? Well, I don't know Patsy that well, but she once looked at me funny. I've been trying to make sure I'm not on her bad side ever since.

Can I be sure? I guess I really don't know if she'll be angry or tell anyone else about my brazen refusal because I don't know her that well and I don't even know who she knows.

How can I find out? I could ask her if she'd be very upset with me if I demurred and explain that I'd love to comply with her wishes, but it would come at a great cost to me.

Okay, say it's true that she'd get mad. So what? I hate the feeling that someone doesn't like me or I've let her down.

What will it cost me to comply (i.e., what is the opportunity cost)? I guess I'd have to weigh whether it is worse to let a near stranger be disappointed or to miss two hours of sleep on a night when I can only get six because I've already agreed to build the sets for my daughter's play, which is scheduled for the very next night.

Bottom line: When I look at it that way, it doesn't make a lot of sense to skip my sleep because I'm scared of Patsy.

Closer—break the news to Patsy: Using compassion and my own, well-justified reasons to refuse, I break it to her gently. I tell Patsy that I fully identify with her need for volunteers and under most circumstances, I'd be delighted to turn out a batch of gooey goodies. Unfortunately, I've already committed to be at the school all evening building sets and won't be able to make it to the grocery store before it closes. But I'd be glad to volunteer for the next time if she can give me a little more notice. To my surprise, Patsy tells me she appreciates that. She was actually surprised by the outpouring of volunteers for this sale and has been worried that no one will step up for the next one scheduled for two weeks from now. I agree to bring a double batch and we're both relieved at the outcome.

If you are a people pleaser, you might benefit from trying your own version of this example, starting with some low-stakes situation. Think of it as a gym where you can try exercising a new "no" muscle. It might also help to do a root cause analysis. Why are you a people pleaser? Try asking yourself "why?" five times and see what comes up. Pleasers need to understand that they have no control over other peoples' opinions. Strive for cheerful indifference. As Terry Cole-

Whitaker says in her book of the same name, what you think of me is none of my business.[6]

Yeah-But—Compared to What?

You've got your dreams and desires, but everywhere you turn, there's an obstacle or problem. Everything looks like a reason you can't get what you want. The yeah-but habit can put you in a continuous inertia loop where eventually you give up altogether and hibernate in the comfortably unsatisfying rut you burrowed into long ago.

If you've made it this far, I hope that means you have crafted a vision that sets you so vibrantly aglow that it is enough to rouse you from your slumber. That picture of what your life could be represents what you are giving up on in order to stay stuck for any number of reasons that may seem quite valid to you. If your buts are getting the better of you, take a page out of Stella's playbook. Her willingness to be alert to different ways of reaching her goals led her to find an unexpected opportunity to open a religious bookstore in her church building. Focus on what you *can* do and do that. Also challenge your buts and see if you can find a way to reframe your situation and make it work for you even in the most unexpected ways. Perhaps, like Stella, you'll find the answer was there all along. Awake to new possibilities.

I'll Get to It Just As Soon As . . .

Martin looks like anything but a procrastinator. He's the senior vice president in charge of several operational units in a large corporation. He is a vision of perpetual motion, in constant demand and always on the go. He is busy from dawn to dusk. The only problem is, he rarely gets anything on *his* list done. He is a bit of a pleaser and does relish the fact that he's the "go-to" guy for many of his colleagues. He loves being in on the action. But as I coached him through an analysis, the root cause of his problem revealed itself to be his proclivity toward procrastination.

Martin is a live-in-the-moment kind of guy, so he really enjoys responding to urgent matters, no matter how unimportant. He likes the drama and feeling needed. As we looked at what was on his list of priorities and how he spent his days, there was a huge disconnect. He was responsible for a number of large initiatives, several of which he'd not even started. All of his activities fit onto the urgent side of his importance/urgency matrix. The good news was that he wasn't wasting any time on unimportant/nonurgent matters. The bad news was that he wasn't spending any time on nonurgent important matters either. Every time a colleague knocked on his door with an urgent request, he reasoned he could get to his own work "tomorrow." Well, his boss referred him to me for coaching when a year full of tomorrows never came and Martin fell significantly behind on his own workload.

If you share Martin's inability to discipline yourself to dig into a large project and keep saying, I'll get to that just as soon as... any number of excuses will do... you need a strategy to get focused. Martin is so social and in the moment that I suggested he seek out one of his colleagues that he keeps helping and ask her to help him put a plan in place to tackle his own projects. Since he loves to respond to a crisis, I recommended he ask his colleague to set several "burning" deadlines and to put regular progress reports on the agenda of his boss's staff meetings so he'd be accountable for meeting them.

Perfectionists

Martin was not the only one in his office whose habits kept him from producing stellar results. When his boss, Richard, interviewed me as a potential executive coach for Martin, I asked him a few questions of my own, only to discover that Richard was a bit of a perfectionist and was rarely satisfied with any work product on its first pass. Without intending to, he was actually contributing to Martin's procrastination. By setting standards that were practically impossible to satisfy, he unwittingly added to Martin's resistance to starting difficult new projects that he knew were likely to fall short of Richard's expectations.

Throughout the time I coached Martin, I checked in regularly with Richard. During this time, Richard did some self-analysis of his own, which revealed a fear of failure at the root of his perfectionism. Always afraid that he wasn't on top of all the emerging trends in his industry, Richard felt that every quarterly board meeting was an oral exam he could fail at any time. His board included some of the greats in his industry, and he worried he couldn't keep up with them, each with his own team of top-tier analysts. He passed his anxiety on to his staff to the point that he undercut their self-confidence and made them fearful of turning in work that he was likely to reject.

Richard's fears were contagious and, ironically, were perpetuating the conditions he feared the most. So we worked on reframing the situation and finding another approach that would work and *feel* better for him and his staff. I pointed out that he and the board of directors were actually on the same team and wanted the same thing, namely for the company to perform well. Their incentives were well aligned. Richard needed to stop looking at the directors as a board of examiners he needed to dazzle with perfect presentations and start looking at them as the rich resource they were.

I suggested he start reaching out to the directors one at a time to see what he could learn from each of them and how they could help his staff design and research their analyses. This strategy accomplished a few important objectives. First, by spending time getting to know the directors, he was building important relationships. As he got better acquainted with each board member, he started to feel more confident that they wanted to help him succeed rather than catch him falling short of expectations. Second, he learned valuable information about his industry that improved the quality of his work. Finally, and perhaps most importantly, he was able to shift the tenor of the board meetings into more of a collaborative discussion of key issues rather than a show and tell that left the directors bored and feeling underutilized by the company. Within a few short months, he felt much more confident in his standing with the board and, over time, he was able to ease up the pressure on his staff, making the workplace much more pleasant and productive.

If you are a perfectionist, you need to accept that you cannot control every outcome and you will never know everything. Remember the serenity prayer and put your efforts where you can have a positive impact.

I'm reminded of a moment of clarity on my yoga mat when I realized that strength is the ability to hold on, but power is the ability to let go. The best any of us can do is to prepare as thoroughly as possible and then find the courage to jump in with both feet.

Conclusion

How They Got Their Glow

"Little by little, one walks far."

—Peruvian proverb

One of the most popular sessions in my longer workshops is the reunion we hold about six weeks after the course ends. Participants come together to report on their successes and struggles. They celebrate one another's achievements and share strategies to overcome obstacles.

The people whose stories fill these pages came to me for courses or coaching with similar goals: to fill their days with more satisfaction, fulfillment, and joy. They wanted to improve their experience at work and at home. They all went through the same process, defining their purpose and creating visions that set them aglow. They lit up at different points and in their own unique way. They made changes, large, medium, and small. They came to improve how they managed the business of their lives and that they did.

Has everyone who has ever taken my courses made improvements? I really can't say. I do everything possible to set people up for long-term success. Life happens and it is entirely possible that some people go back to business as usual. Hopefully, they pull a technique out of their new tool kit when faced with a decision to make or a dilemma to solve, whenever the time is right. The people who come to see me in the months and years following their workshops or coaching do so because they're excited to tell me how they've used what they learned to do something that was meaningful for them.

As I've mentioned before, the framework presented in this book is tidy and structured, but the world we live in can be chaotic and messy. These tools can't always compensate for tough circumstances, but they can help you do the best you can with the cards you've been dealt. Sometimes, they can help you see how to reshuffle the deck and even find some new cards to play. As one example, in this economy, many people feel happy to have any job (if they even have one), let alone one they find gratifying. They have bills to pay and can't afford to take time off to contemplate a more satisfying career. So the workshop provided them with tools and ideas to make their current job more enjoyable. Beyond that, they were able to find ways to incorporate their passions and talents in other aspects of their lives, like Regina, who found so much joy singing in her church choir.

This program can help you find the resilience you need and a new, more productive approach when you have tried something that didn't work out the way you'd hoped. As the Chinese proverb says, if you get up one more time than you fall, you will make it through. You can always go back to the list of potential strategies you developed in step 7 if the first one you tried didn't produce the results you expected.

Consider this your reunion. People take from the experience what they need, when they need it. Some come hoping to make minor adjustments to a life that's already going pretty well. Others are looking for a complete change in direction because they're unhappy with the status quo or their circumstances shift. In a moment, we will take a look at how the people whose stories you've been reading have fared thus far. But your story doesn't end here.

You have just learned a framework and tools that you can use at any time to achieve whatever it is you want or need to do. At this point, are you wondering if you've done enough? Done it right? Pshaw. Right, shmite. Let me remind you that YOU are the expert on you. Only you can answer those questions for yourself. This is not a course that comes with a final exam and a grade on a report card. The program presented in this book is meant to serve you. It is *not* meant to be one more set of expectations for you to fulfill. No "shoulds" here.

This book can serve as a resource for years to come. I hope you have found it useful to think about things in a new way and learned some tricks that help you be more productive and effective—in whatever way benefits you. Only you can be the judge of that.

Tweaks and Transformations

The people in this book have selected the techniques that work for them and have assembled their own custom toolkits to serve their specific needs. I am always delighted to hear some of the interesting ways they have applied the tools to fix their own unique circumstances.

Using Their Tools to Build a Better Situation

One last time, allow me to emphasize just how important it is to write down the elements of this program that mean the most to you somewhere it will be easy for you to access at any time. Your custom closet can serve that purpose, or you are most welcome to use whatever application or technique works for you. Just be sure to find one that does. Then, so you won't forget, schedule time to review it at regular intervals. Telling someone about your plans and committing to keeping them updated on your progress is another excellent way to stay on track. Also, the more you make a practice of using the tools presented here, the more likely they will just become a part of the way you think.

Setting Priorities and Staying on Point

Brandon is the busy executive who used his vision statement to decide if he should accept the invitation to serve on a prestigious corporate board. His picture of success had him available to attend his children's soccer games and special events, so it was clear that joining that board at that particular time was in conflict with his immediate priorities. He found the clarity his vision provided so powerful that he continues to use his tools and filters to maintain awareness and make good decisions. He reasoned that he will likely have another opportunity to serve on a corporate board, but his son would never be eleven again.

He has used the importance/urgency matrix to prioritize projects at work and at home. He has shared his tool kit with his family and colleagues and encourages them to give careful thought to the choices they make. Brandon is a fan of the "big rock" concept presented in step 7 and uses that thinking each morning to determine what he wants to achieve. Then he sticks to the plan as much as circumstances allow.

He had been particularly concerned that his colleagues would look at him askance if he left work during the day to go to an event at his kids' school, so he worked out an ironclad plan to make sure he consistently delivered high-quality work on time and on budget. That plan worked well. He is thriving at work and is home when needed. But something unexpected happened. Far from being looked down upon for making family a priority, he has become a leader in his company and a champion of work–life balance. His colleagues look to him as a role model. Something he feared has actually boosted his career and improved retention and morale in his company. In turn, his personal goals are much easier to achieve.

Keeping Joy on the Agenda

As you saw, the visioning and goal-setting steps provided a powerful framework for Sandra. Her vision statement helped focus her prodigious energy on those initiatives that mattered most to her. Setting priorities helped her see that launching her nonprofit organization, Fertility Within Reach, was an urgent desire. So much so that she launched it in one year, not the five years she had initially envisioned.

Sandra also became more disciplined about managing the projects she and her team took on at work. She developed a full-blown project plan for each initiative, figuring that if it was worth doing, it was worth doing right. The structured approach helped her hold her staff accountable, which was especially important because they were scattered across a few different locations.

Sandra told me that her Business of Life tools helped her do something else that completely transformed her personal life. She now runs every decision through a "joy-to-hassle ratio" analysis. Before agreeing to a request from her family, community, whomever, she asks herself, "Am I going to get any joy out of this?" If the answer is no, she feels no guilt from declining. She wouldn't do anything that wouldn't benefit her business, so why would she do that in her personal life? Her vision statement and a few simple questions help her keep joy on the agenda.

Small Shifts Can Yield Big Dividends

Richard also found that, paradoxically, easing up a bit can make a huge difference in the workplace. He is the corporate executive whose impossibly high standards were inhibiting his staff, who were reluctant to turn in assignments because he was so likely to find fault with them. Richard did a "five whys" analysis to get to the root of his paranoia-driven perfectionism.

Why do I demand perfection from my staff and myself?

I am afraid our analyses fall short of board members' high expectations.

Why (do I fear our analyses will fall short of expectations)?

The board members are industry leaders with access to the most cutting-edge intelligence and economic forecasts and they will expect the same of us.

Why (would they expect that of us)?

I'm not sure, but I assume they would expect me to know what they know.

Why (do I assume they would expect me to know what they know)?

I am afraid to ask them what they expect.

Why (am I afraid to ask them)?

I might look weak since they probably expect me to know what they expect.

When we reviewed his answers, Richard appreciated the irony of his own lack of thoroughness in preparing himself to produce a stellar product. He wasn't holding himself to the same high standard to which he was holding his staff. All out of fear of looking "bad" to his board. He created a great deal of angst for himself and everyone else by managing according to what he imagined might be expected of him. Leadership 101 calls for setting explicit expectations and managing to objective, measurable outcomes. Richard wasn't even managing himself well, since he failed to establish expectations with his board.

I also pointed out to him that his board members were there to be a resource for him and his company, not to trip him up at meetings. Richard needed to create relationships with the directors so he could make the most of this valuable resource and establish an agreement on the best approach to their collective work. Not only had his paranoia stifled his staff's creativity, it deprived the board members of the satisfaction of fully contributing their expertise to benefit the company.

We agreed that Richard would invite one locally based director to lunch each week or set up a phone call if the director was located at a distance. Most board members were pleased to be engaged in this way and were eager to share their advice. Once Richard realized that he had allies and even mentors on the board, he was able to relax in the knowledge that they wanted to see him succeed, not fail.

This simple shift in the way he looked at his board was a game changer. With the knowledge that he could ask for help and advice, he was able to ease up on his staff, letting them be more creative and take some risks. Their performance and morale increased immeasurably. As an added benefit, Richard's intake of ulcer medication went down proportionately. Probably more than anyone, his wife was delighted that he managed to be home for dinner and was in a good mood much more frequently.

Freedom from Fear

Brenda, the would-be manager whose middle school teacher told her she had no ability with numbers, faced down her phobia and enrolled in a college math course en route to pursuing the management career to which she aspired. During the semester, she worked hard, took advantage of every bit of extra help she could get, and joined a study group. During this time, we also looked for ways she could bring more elements of management into her current job. She asked for a project to lead so she could build up her track record and beef up her résumé. Her manager was pleased to see her take the initiative and gratefully put her in charge of overseeing their department's renovations and the process of moving all the faculty and staff to their new space.

The day Brenda showed up in my office to show me her final grade — an A—she was positively beaming. She had shed the shackles that had held her back for years and truly believed there was nothing she couldn't do. After acing the one thing she was sure was beyond her abilities, her confidence soared and she enrolled in a degree program. She loved college life and immersed herself fully in that experience. Rather than exhausting her, school *gave* her energy and she sailed through her program, working day and night to complete it. Tragically, just a few months shy of graduating, she was diagnosed with an aggressive form of cancer. With every ounce of strength and determination she possessed, she earned her bachelor's degree before succumbing to her disease.

At her memorial service, I was filled with grief and gratitude. Brenda faced her fate with grace. She had finally discovered what she was capable of achieving. What's more, she was able to teach her nieces to question anyone who told them there was something they couldn't do. As Brenda learned more about management at school, she had several opportunities to put that knowledge to use at work. Her efforts were appreciated and she found that enormously satisfying right up until the time she was too ill to work any longer. Brenda unchained her melody. She did not die with her song still inside her. And that was enough for her.

Total Reboots

The pain of not pursuing their dreams or making a difference was enough to compel several people to seek wholesale change. They wanted to use their considerable talents more fully and to make their days matter. Despite their professional accomplishments, they were unfulfilled and curious why that was. So I showed them that to achieve *soul-satisfying* success, they needed a plan.

Passion Pushes Past Inertia

Danielle found the courage to leave her lucrative yet soul-sucking career in fashion to pursue her passions when she was laid off from her job. She was able to resist taking another position in the same industry once she realized that her work hadn't incorporated any of the things she truly enjoyed. While she was very nervous about making a living, she finally had the time and mental space to contemplate her options. She started by injecting the free days that stretched before her with some pleasure. Having set goals to take a cooking class and to start preparing home-cooked meals, she got right to it. When she stepped into the cooking school's kitchen, she had that wonderful feeling that she was finally home.

As soon as that course ended, she immediately searched for her next gastronomic adventure and enrolled in a class to learn how to make artisanal chocolates. From the moment she plunged her hands into the warm liquid confection, she knew she was literally dipping into her dreams. This was *it*. Danielle had stumbled on a way to combine her artistic skills, business acumen, and love of all things culinary. She took the entrepreneurial plunge. She has never looked back. Her website states the principles that fueled the goals she set for her enterprise: "Our passion for recapturing small production, sane business practices, and quality of life and product defines us."

Her story doesn't end there. With what she considers a kind of cosmic confirmation that all is right with her world, she received an e-mail from a woman who had lost her job and wanted to strike out on her own. Danielle recounted the tale:

I called her and we chatted for a while. She was in New York and her dad had forwarded an article written about me from

South Shore Magazine. Two weeks later I received an e-mail from my college roommate thanking me for being so kind to her best friend. Her friend told her she had spoken with a woman in Massachusetts who had started a chocolate business. She knew it had to be me. It was a crazy small world moment that I just loved. It makes me feel that I am doing exactly what I should be doing and we are connected to certain people for a reason.

Danielle is having the time of her life and business couldn't be better. In fact, I recently logged on to her website to find a picture of a chocolate man wearing a Santa Claus hat and waving a white flag. It said, "We surrender! We can't make it fast enough…(to guarantee delivery on new orders) before Christmas." This statement is evidence of her adhering to the principles that define her business.

She has also hung onto her razor-sharp wit as she relayed her adventures with a photo shoot for yet another magazine feature: "They sent Manolo Blahniks but my bunioned feet would not fit in them so I had to wear my real chocolate shoes, which are cork-soled clogs. Hmmm…could I dip in Manolos? Anyway, it was fabulous to be fawned over by hair and makeup stylists for the day. I felt like a princess. A princess in clogs."

Danielle's renaissance began when she took her first cooking class. If you are looking for a change, consider following your heart and doing something you love—just because you love doing it. You're practically guaranteed to have a good time and you just never know where it might lead you.

Time to Please Me

Like Danielle, spending time considering his passions convinced our people-pleasing lawyer, Jim, to re-chart his course and get off the path he'd embarked on to please his parents. While a law career wasn't what he'd envisioned for himself, he thought that he would be able to find a niche in that field where he could fulfill his desire to connect with his clients and have a meaningful impact on their lives. But the reality of legal practice did not fit his idealistic notions of how he could make a difference while making a living.

When Jim looked at what he liked about his legal work, he realized that it was counseling his clients, mastering an extensive body of information, and writing complex legal briefs that brought him pleasure. But he found that working in a corporate environment and focusing so much attention on billable hours left him feeling spiritually bankrupt. He didn't mind the tasks he had to perform, but he felt like a fish out of water in that setting.

Jim found a new direction when he focused on his mission. He had no trouble identifying where his talents and passions intersected with the needs of individuals and the world.[1] He loved counseling people, reading and writing on spiritual topics, and working with nonprofit organizations. Somewhere deep inside him, he knew what he felt called to do. He wanted to be a rabbi, trading in torts for Torah. And he's in good company. Jim called to tell me that he knew of at least six other attorneys who were pursuing the rabbinate at his seminary. Each day he's in school, he feels sure he is in the right place. And while he's finally following his own heart, his parents couldn't be more pleased. Who knew?

Who AM I Anyway?

Truth be told, I take the time in my courses to teach about guiding principles mostly as an affirmation of peoples' good intentions. This exercise is usually just a quick listing of the core values that fuel our behavior. It doesn't usually prompt major changes. It just makes everyone conscious of what drives them so they feel good about their motivations before they move on to the next step. That is, until I met Miranda.

Miranda, the corporate CEO we first encountered in the mission step, was in her late fifties when her beloved, elderly Chihuahua, Carmen, died. As time went on, Miranda's grief deepened and she felt seriously depressed. She wasn't in the habit of allowing herself time to notice, let alone indulge, her feelings. Now, however, she was so overwhelmed with sorrow that she did the unthinkable: she cancelled her attendance at a board meeting and spent a few unscheduled days at home for the first time in recent memory.

On a long, solitary walk on the beach, she made a major discovery about herself: she was an addict. While some people turn to alcohol or cocaine, Miranda's drug of choice was activity. Now, with three days on her hands with little to do but think, she couldn't avoid her emotions. She realized that Carmen's death was so devastating because not only did she lose her constant companion, she lost the only friend who ever loved her unconditionally. She felt angry, alone in the company of others, and afraid she would die a bitter, bejeweled old woman. The vision of where she was headed frightened her so intensely she did something else she would have found unthinkable a few short weeks earlier. She asked for help.

Miranda knew that a colleague on one of her boards was coming to me for coaching and she decided to give it a try herself. She was still quite upset when she arrived for her first session. We decided to start by examining the source of her distress so her plans could address the root cause rather than the symptoms. Once she started paying attention, her insights flowed freely.

Her parents were very traditional and very well off. Her father was a prominent businessman and her mother was very active in civic affairs as a volunteer. They lavished Miranda with gifts and her brother with attention. When she was a young girl, her parents expected Miranda to have impeccable manners and to marry well some day. They invested most of their parenting energy on her brother, whom they groomed to take over his father's company—something Miranda would have liked very much for herself. She rebelled by getting an education and working her way up the corporate ladder. She was determined to show her parents what a girl could do and hoped to gain their admiration in the process. Her behavior didn't meet their expectations of what was becoming for their precious jewel, and they were rarely impressed by her accomplishments. She was promoted, won awards, and commanded a huge salary, and still her parents never offered their approval. Frustrated, she became a shrill, demanding taskmaster prone to legendary outbursts of temper.

Before we got going in earnest on developing her personal strategic plan, Miranda required more data. An exacting executive, she wanted a full dossier before she was ready to tackle the project of her life. So, we performed a 360-degree evaluation in which I confidentially interviewed those all around her at work and in the community. The results were sobering. She wasn't surprised that many of the professionals I interviewed thought she was tough and highly competitive. However, she was truly pained to find out the administrative staff secretly referred to her as "Cruella Deville" because she would "bite their heads off" if she didn't like the way they carried out an assignment. Miranda was quite fond of these young women and had no idea that they felt that way about her.

This revelation haunted her as she began the planning process. Her "ahas" started right from the beginning as we reviewed her life's purpose. She'd never given much thought to her mission other than showing her parents how wrong they were about what a girl could do. She'd long ago proven that she could succeed in the male-dominated business world, but that never filled the void. Yet she kept on going after promotions and honors—all sorts of outward validation of her worth. Like an addict, she was seeking to fill a hole in her soul with awards and accolades. It didn't work. She needed to make a difference.

Her experiences, coupled with the pain of learning that her young colleagues disliked her so intensely, led her to believe her life's mission had something to do with creating opportunities for other women to develop their full potential and thrive in the workplace. Working on her vision statement and looking at her strengths helped her flesh out how she might approach that mission.

For Miranda, who did whatever it took to whomever was in her path on the way to the corner office, stopping to contemplate the principles that would guide her actions going forward was a transformational exercise. She committed to fostering empowerment, excellence, opportunity, honesty, integrity, and generosity in herself and

others. Her newly espoused values clearly lit the path she would follow to the end of her career.

With this important groundwork completed, setting priorities was
fairly simple for such a consummate businesswoman, as was developing
strategies to achieve her new goals. She knew how to mobilize resources
to get results. She created a plan and started a program to help disadvan-
taged young women prepare to enter the workplace. She held them to
exacting standards, but most were able to rise to her high expectations.
Miranda worked directly with several of the girls and found that watching them gain confidence, skills, and, ultimately, jobs was extremely
satisfying. While I can't say Miranda turned into a marshmallow, her
edges have softened a great deal. Her face looks more serene and far less
pinched. And she's held on to a secretary for several years, after having
gone through more assistants than Murphy Brown.

Now Miranda finds much more satisfaction giving out scholarships
and awards than she ever experienced in receiving them. She finds
fulfillment in giving what she never received from her own parents—
the gift of listening to what these girls really want and helping them to
achieve their dreams. In turn, with each young woman she helps, she
is healing her own wounds.

Miranda called me recently to tell me she had just received the
most meaningful award of her career. A few of the young women
she had helped along the way chipped in to buy her a pewter bowl to
thank her for seeing their potential and insisting they stick with the
rigorous program until they graduated and secured employment. She
was particularly touched that a young woman whom she helped to
land her first job presented the gift. Miranda had a first of her own that
day: she shed her very first tears of joy.

Built a Better Balance

Countless people come for classes or coaching when they feel like
their lives are out of balance. For many, that means spending so much
time on work that there is little time left over for other priorities. The

administrative and time management skills they learn help them become more efficient. But often it is the act of committing those other priorities to paper and making a plan to address them that allows the real shifts to take place. There is something about the visual experience of seeing your priorities mapped out that snaps that vague sense of imbalance into sharp relief. Once you can see where your issues lie, you can make choices that serve you better.

He Finally Fit in Some Fun

Paul is the finance manager who took my Business of Life course after relocating for his new position. In class, he had a very serious demeanor, dour almost, and made a point of emphasizing that he was taking the course to sharpen his planning skills so he could dazzle his new boss. He never participated in discussions about the "softer" issues that engaged his classmates. So he surprised us all when it came time to talk about goal setting. He realized when he looked at his custom life closet that he had put all of his eggs in the career basket and had not made a priority of his relationships, health, or place in the community. This hit him especially hard as he thought about what it meant to live in a new city where he didn't know anyone. Frankly, he found it rather depressing.

He immediately set some goals to get more exercise and to meet new people. And he wanted to have some fun. Paul had always liked volleyball, so when his local adult education center organized a team, he joined. After their first game, a rousing victory, he invited his teammates out for a celebratory drink. In the weeks that followed, the team often went out after games and he made a few new friends whom he met for meals and movies. Paul's newly balanced life paid dividends for him on the job as well.

With a life outside of work, Paul had something to talk about with his colleagues besides budgets and balance sheets. His colleagues found him more likable. Once he loosened up, his colleagues started to include him in their social activities. They were also more willing to collaborate with him on projects. The quality of his work life *and* work products improved when he focused on leading a more balanced existence.

Metabolic Multitasking

Mark is the attorney who sought out coaching once he made partner in his law firm. Years of a singular focus on getting promoted had taken its toll on his health and social life. He was ready to get back into shape and back in the game. He used all of the prioritization matrices to establish an exercise program that would also serve his goal to be more social. He had settled on jogging a few days a week with friends as part of his routine. When his sister invited him to participate in a ten-kilometer race to raise money for kids with autism, he readily agreed. It served a cause that mattered to him and was a catalyst to get him off the couch and on the road.

Using his natural ability to organize groups, he put together an e-mail distribution list and invited several friends to meet him at the appointed time and place for his planned runs. He encouraged everyone to invite their friends and post their plans as well. Before long, there were more than thirty people on the e-mail list and a dozen or more showed up for most of the morning runs. Several signed up to participate in the autism race as well. At our last meeting, Mark told me he had just met an intriguing woman on one of his morning runs. With a twinkle in his eye he said, "I'm thinking of running a few extra days a week. You know, to get in shape faster."

Starting with Their Strengths

When they first set out to start Our Space, Inc. to provide art therapy programs for children affected by cancer, Peggy and Gail were overwhelmed by the myriad steps required to launch their new organization. They started small, with tasks that appealed to their artistic sensibilities and drew on their strengths. But they well knew they lacked the business skills and other things they needed to make Our

Space a reality. Their SWOT analysis (strengths, weaknesses, opportunities, and threats) defined the gulf that stood between them and fulfilling their vision.

Just when they needed it most, Lee Ann appeared, ready to bridge the gap. She was the talented program manager who told me of her desire to use her artistic and planning skills to help people with cancer. As you saw in the SWOT step, her skills and Peggy and Gail's vision were the missing pieces in each other's puzzles. I was delighted to make an introduction and witness the impressive results of this collaboration. Lee Ann guided Gail and Peggy through the process of creating a business plan, setting up an advisory board, and incorporating Our Space. She provided the structure that was essential to harnessing their creative energy and channeling it into practical action that produced tangible results. In turn, Lee Ann found a worthy outlet for her organizational gifts. Clearly, her talents and passions collided with a real need in the world.

All the while, Gail and Peggy continue to draw on their strengths to grow the program and work toward building a permanent space. With Lee Ann's help, they've hosted several successful fundraisers showcasing Gail's comedic talents and artwork they and their many friends created. They offer their art therapy programs in numerous hospitals and other settings while they continue to march toward their vision of opening a dedicated space. Connecting with patients and supporting their families in these challenging moments brings them great satisfaction, infusing their path with joy and inspiration.

Do you think they were just lucky to find each other? As the saying goes, luck is what happens when preparation meets opportunity. Peggy and Gail were so passionately committed to finding meaning in their own struggles with cancer that they kept looking for ways to make it happen, even when their dream seemed impossibly beyond their reach. They told everyone they knew about their vision. Their friends connected them with others who could help bring it to life. And, as we've seen in other examples, a compelling vision makes others want to be a part of it.

As for Lee Ann, corralling these artistic types could be a challenge at times, but it was enormously exciting to guide them and see their vision take shape. Helping kids with their art projects in those early days gave beautiful expression to her desire to work with cancer patients. Not long after Our Space hit its stride, Lee Ann landed a great job in risk management, the field she missed after leaving her previous position to care for her aunt. Her employer allows enough flexibility for volunteer work. Now she's happily engaging her heart *and* head, using her gifts to make a difference.

Steadying the Boat in Stormy Seas

Thelma is the hospital department head whose goal was to stop yelling at her family. Her Business of Life classmates wouldn't let her get away with her proposed strategy: trying to pretend she wasn't angry when her husband and son left their dirty socks on the floor. She was grateful to her colleagues for pushing her to be honest with herself and confront what was really causing her such distress. And to value herself enough to put herself on her list of priorities. She shared her powerful story when I interviewed her some three years after her course ended:

> Your class couldn't have come at a better time in my life. It was about a year before my world fell apart, and if I hadn't learned those skills and had time to practice them and make them my own, I don't know how I would have managed. Really.

Thelma recalled her class project and how touched she was when her classmates challenged her with so much compassion. Her closet and calendar exercises showed her how she'd left herself out of every equation, putting everyone and everything ahead of her own needs. She was exhausted. Her goal for that group exercise was to stop yelling at her family. Her strategy was to just forget how angry it made her when her son and husband took off their socks in the living room and just left them on the floor. For such a strategic thinker, that wasn't much of a strategy, so I instructed her do a root cause analysis on why this situation upset her so much.

This exercise showed Thelma that the socks bothered her so much because they were a symptom of a much larger issue.

With her new knowledge, the class encouraged Thelma to talk to her son, who was thirteen at the time, and she put up a chart that rewarded him for every day the living room was free of his socks. He lost a point for every day the socks (or hats or whatever) were there. It took him close to a year, but he earned enough points to get the game system he wanted.

But Thelma discovered her challenges went much deeper as she recounted in her interview. "My husband was another story. It turns out he was having an affair and my son found out about it. My husband insisted he keep it to himself. My son (who knew the socks were the least of his worries) became seriously depressed because he felt powerless to do anything about it. To make a long story short, he ended up in the hospital to get treated for his anger and depression. It was there he found the courage to tell me about my husband's affair...I threw my husband out that very day."

Thelma took responsibility for her part in this family drama and set out immediately to chart a more productive course for herself and her children. She recalled that she could have fallen apart, but found that the Business of Life tools showed her there was another way out of this situation. She knew her kids needed her to be strong and steady. Work was her safe place where she was in charge, respected, and successful. She needed for that to remain the case so she revised her personal strategic plan. When Thelma got to the SWOT, she realized that she'd contributed to her son's depression by not being stronger about holding him to higher standards of respectful behavior. She felt that contributed to his poor self-esteem. She realized, thanks to her classmates, the sock chart was the first time she'd really held him accountable for his behavior. "He needed me to do more of that. I knew I couldn't do that without building my own sense of self-worth."

Thelma re-read her class notes and what I'd said about being present. That led her to a yoga class that is all about cultivating awareness. She reported that she learned how to be present, aware, and able to cope with life as a single mother and so many transitions. And she learned to put taking care of her own wellbeing on the to do list.

Maybe most of all, the planning tools you taught me helped me to be viewed as a strong leader in the hospital. I know I have the respect and support of the doctors I work with and that's crucial to my sense of self-worth. Work was the one constant positive thing during the year from hell. The strategic planning structure made it easy to evaluate even the most complicated project and to break it down into doable steps.

Now, everything feels doable.

Slow, Steady Success

Stella, who broke her "yeah-but" habit when she established the religious bookstore and cafe she'd always dreamed of, provided an update a few years after taking her class. She came to her workshop assuming her goal was beyond her reach because she couldn't afford to quit her day job and lose her benefits. So how would she ever realize this ambition? Stella learned to question her limiting beliefs and look beyond the "buts" to find what's possible. As soon as she opened herself up to seeing novel opportunities to fulfill her aspiration, she found a way to do it. "Your course was a catalyst for me... Thank you. The bookstore and cafe is my joy. Although open on weekends only, I expanded to a larger space and increased my product line."

She is working on a new website where she plans to sell T-shirt designs that her graphic designer son is creating exclusively for her shop. He is helping her with marketing to boost sales. Stella considers her bookstore a work in progress that is "moving in the right direction (ever so slowly). In the meantime the café is holding its own... The fellowship is amazing."

And They Lived...Ever After

The people featured in the sections that follow make a regular practice of reviewing their closets to ensure they stay on track. It reminds them to continue with their productive strategies or take on new priorities as they achieve goals or their circumstances shift.

Gratefully Ever After

You met Regina in the goal-setting step. She's the IT project manager who had fallen into some unhealthy habits, such as dining on fast food, after having her first child. Despite having a satisfying job and a family she adored, Regina was exhausted and prone to bouts of depression. Among others, her goals included starting an exercise regimen and setting a good example for her young daughter.

Regina has ditched the fast-food drive-through in favor of stopping at the salad bar on nights she doesn't have time to cook. She set modest fitness goals and, as a result, has had no difficulty meeting them. In fact, she looks forward to her evening walks with her daughter, who is now four years old. Steadily, her weight has dropped and her moods have lifted.

With more energy and more confidence in her ability to manage, she had a second daughter (whom she straps into her baby carrier for those walks) and is taking a graduate-level course one day a week. Regina continues to sing in her church choir and loves everything about it—the music, friendships, and spending time in the building that always makes her feel divinely inspired. Despite the ups and downs that go with being a working mother, Regina has always been appreciative of her many gifts. Now she has added a practice of a gratitude meditation during her morning commute on the train so she never loses sight of her great fortune.

Consciously Ever After

Angie is the bank vice president who left her prestigious job to raise her children and, ironically, busied herself with volunteer work to the point where she didn't have the time she wanted to be able to spend with her children. Her identity was so caught up with being respected for her business know-how that she had a hard time embracing her role as full-time mother. However, that's just what she longed to be— for now.

The key for Angie was becoming conscious of what was driving her decisions. For some time, she'd convinced herself she was taking on so many volunteer assignments because she was the only one who could do them well enough. She was, after all, a bank vice president. Once she did her time and emotion study, she could see she was spending more of her time nurturing her ego than her children. Her goals and the way she invested her time were not in harmony. She very much wanted to help her kids with their homework and to see them excel academically. In addition, she wanted to be the one to drive them to their extracurricular activities. Family dinners were also a priority for her.

Once she confronted the reality of what she was doing, it was simple for her to realign her calendar with her priorities. She wanted to remain active in her community, but she became far more selective about the work she accepted. She still checks her custom closet now and then and limits herself to no more than one meeting per day with rare exception. Hoping to return to work when her kids are older, Angie gives priority to serving on boards that will help keep her professional network active. Until then, she is present and fully committed to her current position: mom.

Joyfully Ever After

As you saw in the vision step, Bruce's career was going well and he adored his wife and two little girls. Still, he felt a vague dissatisfaction when he came to his Business of Life course to sharpen his business skills and get to the bottom of his discontent. When he struggled to write his vision statement, he made some important discoveries. He knew that he and his wife, Mara, wanted to have a third child, though they didn't know how that could fit into their already crowded schedules. As he envisioned his ideal life, it was full of the love, laughter, and silliness he and Mara had enjoyed as a young couple. But as their days filled with more and more responsibility at work and logistics at home, their focus had shifted away from simply having fun with each other. Bruce worried that his circumstances made his vision infeasible to realize, so he was reluctant to write it down. I instructed him not to worry about *how* he would fulfill his vision or to limit his ambitions at that point. Cultivating some awareness was key to his ability to make some adjustments.

First, Bruce noted that he had yet to cut back on the extra "face time" he had started putting in years ago to establish his career, even though his star had already risen. Second, just writing his vision statement clarified for him the source of his other main issue. He and Mara had settled into a routine that did not make time for them to connect romantically and just enjoy each other. He didn't even need the five whys to tell him that they didn't giggle nearly as often as they used to.

With that kind of clarity, the fixes weren't hard to identify. His time and emotion exercise gave him the opportunity to reshuffle his work schedule now that he no longer needed to attend all the committee meetings that had helped establish his leadership position. He would reinvest that newly liberated time toward his family goals. Mara was overjoyed when Bruce proposed hiring a babysitter so they could go out every Saturday night with the simple goal of having fun and remembering to love each other.

One of the sweetest moments of my career came when Bruce dropped by for a surprise visit about a year after his course ended. He stuck his head in the door, a goofy grin stretching from one ear to the other. Then he stepped all the way in and revealed the bundle in his arms. With as much pride and joy as can fit on a single face, Bruce said, "Meet Zoe." Then we both laughed until we cried.

Epilogue

Be on Your Merry Way

Like all these people, you can use your closet and tools for years to come. You can use these strategic planning steps to structure any undertaking and optimize its chances for success. With regular practice, this just becomes part of how you think. There is no need to leave your dreams to chance. If you haven't already, this is a good time to put monthly reminders on your calendar to keep your priorities up to date and track your progress.

Life is a wild, wondrous adventure and you never know what awaits you around the next bend. Stick to your plans as long as they continue to guide you toward the results you desire, but don't get so attached to them that they constrain you. Stay alert to changes around you and adapt as needed. Be open to new possibilities.

My mission is to help you to use your gifts and make your dreams come true. You have defined your destination, selected a route, and figured out what you need to fill your days with pleasure. You are well prepared for your journey, ready to step onto your path with confidence. Have a great trip and keep in touch. It will be my true joy to hear about your triumphs. You are about to change your own little corner of the world.

Endnotes

Introduction

1. *U.S. News and World Report,* 2012–2013, accessed December 14, 2012, http://health.usnews.com/best-hospitals/area/ma/massachusetts-general-hospital-6140430

2. Lester R. Bittel, *The Nine Master Keys of Management* (New York: McGraw-Hill, 1972), 123.

3. Henry David Thoreau, *Walden* (New York: Thomas Y. Crowell and Company, 1910), 118.

4. Abigail Klein Leichman, "Supportive Bosses Help Reduce Employee Sick Days," Israel 21C, March 18, 2012, accessed December 14, 2012, http://israel21c.org/health/research/supportive-bosses-help-reduce-employee-sick-days/.

5. *Merriam-Webster Dictionary,* accessed February 9, 2013, http://www.merriam-webster.com/dictionary/organize.

Step I

1. Benjamin Franklin, *Benjamin Franklin, Wit and Wisdom* (White Plains, NY: Peter Pauper Press, 1998), 19.

2. Matthew Kelly, *Perfectly Yourself—9 Lessons for Enduring Happiness* (New York: Ballantine, 2006), 180.

3. Abraham. H. Maslow, *Motivation and Personality, Second Edition* (New York: Harper and Row, 1970), 46.

4. Dick Richards, *Is Your Genius at Work? Four Key Questions to Ask Before Your Next Career Move* (Mountain View, CA: Davies-Black Publishing, 2005), 122.

Step 2

1. Lewis Carroll, *The Annotated Alice: The Definitive Version* (New York: W.W. Norton and Company, 2000), 66.

2. Mike Robbins, *Be Yourself, Everyone Else Is Already Taken* (San Francisco: Jossey Bass, 2009).

3. Image can be found at http://web.mit.edu/persci/gaz/gaz-teaching/flash/koffka-movie.swf. Reproduced with permission from Edward H. Adelson.

Step 3

1. Michael P. Wright, *The Coaches' Chalkboard* (Lincoln, NE: Writers Club Press, 2003), 39.

Step 4

1. Laurence Chang, *Wisdom of the Soul: Five Millennia of Prescriptions for Spiritual Healing* (Washington, DC: Gnosophia Publishers, 2006), 565.

2. Jimmy Dean, *Thirty Years of Sausage, Fifty Years of Ham: Jimmy Dean's Own Story* (New York: Penguin Books, 2004), 7.

Step 5

1. Jim Collins, *Good to Great* (New York, HarperCollins, 2001).

2. Gail Matthews, Goals Research Summary, http://www.dominican.edu/academics/ahss/undergraduate-programs-1/psych/faculty/fulltime/gailmatthews/researchsummary2.pdf, accessed November 4, 2012.

3. Heidi Grant Halvorson, Ph.D., *Succeed* (New York: Hudson Street Press, 2010).

Step 6

1. Annie Dillard, *The Writing Life* (New York: Harper and Row, 1989), 32.

2. James O'Toole, *Creating the Good Life: Applying Aristotle's Wisdom to Find Meaning and Happiness* (Emmaus, PA: Rodale, 2005), 194.

3. Mark Twain, *The Wit and Wisdom of Mark Twain: A Book of Quotations* (Mineola, NY: Dover Publications, 1999), 47.

4. "E-mails 'Hurt IQ More Than Pot'," CNN.com, accessed November 15, 2012, http://www.cnn.com/2005/WORLD/europe/04/22/text.iq/.

5. Mahatma Gandhi, *Inspiring Thoughts* (Delhi: Rajpal & Sons, 2009), 65.

6. David Allen, *Getting Things Done* (New York: Penguin Group, 2003).

Step 7

1. Dennis T. Jaffe and Cynthia D. Scott, *Take This Job and Love It* (New York: Simon and Schuster, 1988), 161. Reproduced with permission.

Step 8

1. Lao-Tzu, *Tao Te Ching: The New Translation from Tao Te Ching: The Definitive Edition,* translated by Jonathan Star (New York: Penguin Group, 2001), 83.

2. Robert Maurer, Ph.D., *One Small Step Can Change Your Life the Kaizen Way* (New York: Workman Publishing Company, 2004).

3. "Mind Trip: Journey into the Brain," from the film, *Wired to Win: Surviving the Tour de France,* accessed on December 6, 2012, http://www.wiredtowinthe movie.com/mindtrip_xml.html.

4. Tom Peters, *Thriving on Chaos: Handbook for a Management Revolution* (New York: Excel/A California Limited Partnership, 1987), 97.

5. Anthony St. Peter, *The Greatest Quotations of All Time* (www.Xlibris.com. Xlibris, 2010), 598.

6. Terry Cole-Whitaker, *What You Think of Me Is None of My Business* (New York: Penguin, 1979).

Conclusion

1. Matthew Kelly, *Perfectly Yourself—9 Lessons for Enduring Happiness* (New York: Ballantine, 2006), 180.

References

Adelson, ELII. "Lightness Perception and Lightness Illusions." In the *New Cognitive Neurosciences*, Second Edition. Edited by M. Gazzanig. Cambridge, MA: MIT Press, 2009.

Allen, David. *Getting Things Done*. New York: Penguin Group, 2003.

Bittel, Lester R. *The Nine Master Keys of Management*. New York: McGraw-Hill, 1972.

Carroll, Lewis. *The Annotated Alice: The Definitive Version*. New York: W.W. Norton and Company, 2000.

Chang, Laurence. *Wisdom of the Soul: Five Millennia of Prescriptions for Spiritual Healing*. Washington, DC: Gnosophia Publishers, 2006.

CNN.com. "E-mails 'Hurt IQ More Than Pot'" Accessed November 15, 2012. http://www.cnn.com/2005/WORLD/europe/04/22/text.iq/.

Cole-Whitaker, Terry. *What You Think of Me Is None of My Business*. New York: Penguin, 1979.

Collins, Jim. *Good to Great*. New York, HarperCollins, 2001.

Dean, Jimmy. *Thirty Years of Sausage, Fifty Years of Ham: Jimmy Dean's Own Story*. New York: Penguin Books, 2004.

Dillard, Annie. *The Writing Life*. New York: Harper and Row, 1989.

Franklin, Benjamin. *Benjamin Franklin, Wit and Wisdom*. White Plains, NY: Peter Pauper Press, 1998.

Gandhi, Mahatma. *Inspiring Thoughts*. Delhi: Rajpal & Sons, 2009.

Halvorson Heidi Grant. *Succeed*. New York: Hudson Street Press, 2010.

Jaffe, Dennis T., and Cynthia D. Scott. *Take This Job and Love It*. New York: Simon and Schuster, 1988.

Kelly, Matthew. *Perfectly Yourself—9 Lessons for Enduring Happiness*. New York: Ballantine, 2006.

Lao-Tzu. *Tao Te Ching: The New Translation from Tao Te Ching: The Definitive Edition*. Translated by Jonathan Star. New York: Penguin Group, 2001, 83.

Leichman, Abigail Klein. "Supportive Bosses Help Reduce Employee Sick Days." Israel 21C, March 18, 2012. Accessed December 14, 2012. http://israel21c.org/health/research/supportive-bosses-help-reduce-employee-sick-days/.

Maslow, Abraham. H. *Motivation and Personality, Second Edition*. New York: Harper and Row, 1970.

Matthews, Gail. *Goals Research Summary*. Accessed November 4, 2012. http://www.dominican.edu/academics/ahss/undergraduate-programs-1/psych/faculty/fulltime/gailmatthews/researchsummary2.pdf.

Maurer, Robert. *One Small Step Can Change Your Life the Kaizen Way*. New York: Workman Publishing Company, 2004.

Menon, PK. *The Urgent/Important Matrix*. Accessed March 1, 2013. http://driven.pkmenon.com/the-urgent-important-matrix/.

Merriam-Webster Dictionary, online edition. Accessed February 9, 2013. http://www.merriam-webster.com/dictionary/organize.

O'Toole, James. *Creating the Good Life: Applying Aristotle's Wisdom to Find Meaning and Happiness*. Emmaus, PA: Rodale, 2005.

Peters, Tom. *Thriving on Chaos: Handbook for a Management Revolution*. New York: Excel/A California Limited Partnership, 1987.

Richards, Dick. *Is Your Genius at Work? Four Key Questions to Ask Before Your Next Career Move*. Mountain View, CA: Davies-Black Publishing, 2005.

Robbins, Mike. *Be Yourself, Everyone Else Is Already Taken*. San Francisco: Jossey Bass, 2009.

St. Peter, Anthony. *The Greatest Quotations of All Time*. Xlibris, 2010. Xlibris.com.

Thoreau, Henry David. *Walden*. New York: Thomas Y. Crowell and Company, 1910.

Twain, Mark. *The Wit and Wisdom of Mark Twain: A Book of Quotations*. Mineola, NY: Dover Publications, 1999.

U.S. News and World Report, 2012–2013. "Massachusetts General Hospital." Accessed December 14, 2012. http://health.usnews.com/best-hospitals/area/ma/massachusetts-general-hospital-6140430.

Wired to Win: Surviving the Tour de France. "Mind Trip: Journey into the Brain." Accessed December 6, 2012. http://www.wiredtowinthemovie.com/mindtrip_xml.html.

Wright, Michael P. *The Coaches' Chalkboard*. Lincoln, NE: Writers Club Press, 2003.

Index

What's Next?

If you have enjoyed *The Joy of Strategy*, I invite you to connect personally so I can help you create a business plan and make it come to life. There are several ways to do this:

- Visit my website allisonrimm.com to:
  - Sign up for our newsletter filled with tips, tools, and inspiring stories of success and resilience
  - Connect with me on LinkedIn
  - Follow me on Twitter
- Participate in a workshop
- Sponsor any of our professional development programs in your workplace
- Work with one of our coaches for one-on-one guidance with your business plan for life
- Hire our team of consultants to help you develop and execute your organization's strategic plan
- Engage us to help you plan and facilitate your next management retreat
- Invite me to speak at an upcoming event

Go to allisonrimm.com to find out more about these and other offerings.

- Join me at JoyofStrategy.com, where you will find tips, tools, resources, and inspiration to stay on track in business and in life.

- Let me know about your triumphs and challenges. Write to me at allison@allisonrimm.com to ask a question, tell your story, or share a tip that helped you get around a roadblock or take advantage of an interesting opportunity.   I will answer as many questions as I can and will feature selected stories and answer questions in upcoming blog posts and newsletters.

I sincerely hope that you have found the inspiration and practical advice you need to make your dreams come true. It will be my great joy to hear from you.